Apuleius *Metamorpnoses* V

The following titles are available from Bloomsbury for the OCR
specifications in Latin and Greek

Apuleius *Metamorphoses* V: A Selection, with introduction, commentary
notes and vocabulary by Stuart R. Thomson
Cicero *Philippic* II: A Selection, with introduction, commentary notes and
vocabulary by Christopher Tanfield
Horace *Odes*: A Selection, with introduction, commentary notes and
vocabulary by John Godwin
Horace *Satires*: A Selection, with introduction, commentary notes and
vocabulary by John Godwin
Ovid *Amores* II: A Selection, with introduction, commentary notes and
vocabulary by Alfred Artley
Tacitus *Histories* I: A Selection, with introduction by
Ellen O'Gorman and commentary notes and vocabulary by
Benedict Gravell
Virgil *Aeneid* XI: A Selection, with introduction, commentary notes and
vocabulary by Ashley Carter

OCR Anthology for Classical Greek AS and A Level, covering the
prescribed texts by Aristophanes, Euripides, Herodotus, Homer, Plato and
Xenophon, with introduction, commentary notes and vocabulary by
Stephen Anderson, Rob Colborn, Neil Croally, Charlie Paterson,
Chris Tudor and Claire Webster

Supplementary resources for these volumes can be found at
www.bloomsbury.com/OCR-editions OCR-editions-2019–2021
Please type the URL into your web browser and follow the instructions to
access the Companion Website. If you experience any problems, please
contact Bloomsbury at academicwebsite@bloomsbury.com

Apuleius *Metamorphoses* V: A Selection

11–24

With introduction, commentary notes and
vocabulary by Stuart R. Thomson

BLOOMSBURY ACADEMIC

LONDON • NEW YORK • OXFORD • NEW DELHI • SYDNEY

BLOOMSBURY ACADEMIC
Bloomsbury Publishing Plc
50 Bedford Square, London, WC1B 3DP, UK

BLOOMSBURY, BLOOMSBURY ACADEMIC and the Diana logo are trademarks
of Bloomsbury Publishing Plc

First published in Great Britain 2018

Cover image: Bildarchiv Monheim GmbH / Alamy Stock Photo

A catalogue record for this book is available from the British Library.

Library of Congress Cataloging-in-Publication Data
Names: Apuleius, author. | Thomson, Stuart, editor, writer of added commentary.
Title: Metamorphoses V : a selection, V, 11-24 / with introduction, commentary
notes and vocabulary by Stuart R. Thomson.
Description: London ; New York : Bloomsbury Academic, an imprint of
Bloomsbury Publishing, 2018. | Text in Latin; introduction and commentary in
English. | Includes bibliographical references.
Identifiers: LCCN 2017049470| ISBN 9781350010277 (pbk.) |
ISBN 9781350010284 (epub)
Subjects: LCSH: Apuleius. Metamorphoses. | Apuleius. Psyche et Cupido.
Classification: LCC PA6207 .M33 2018 | DDC 873/.01–dc23 LC record
available at https://lccn.loc.gov/2017049470

ISBN: PB: 978-1-3500-1027-7
       ePDF: 978-1-3500-1029-1
       eBook: 978-1-3500-1028-4

Typeset by RefineCatch Limited, Bungay, Suffolk

To find out more about our authors and books visit www.bloomsbury.com
and sign up for our newsletters.

Contents

Preface

The text and notes found in this volume are designed to guide any student who has mastered Latin up to GCSE level and wishes to read a selection of Apuleius' text of the *Metamorphoses* in the original.

The edition is, however, particularly designed to support students who are reading Apuleius' text in preparation for OCR's A-level Latin examination June 2020–June 2021. The extract chosen for the examination forms the core of the tale of Cupid and Psyche, one of the most famous stories embedded within the *Metamorphoses*. Apuleius is chiefly famous for being one of the great prose stylists of the Latin language: trained as an orator, educated as a philosopher, and deeply conscious of the literary heritage of the Latin language, Apuleius' exuberance, playfulness and emotional effect can only be appreciated through a close reading and accurate understanding of his original language, coupled with a nuanced grasp of the tradition within which he was writing.

This edition contains a detailed introduction to the context of the *Metamorphoses*, supported by an in-depth examination of Apuleius' literary techniques and a glossary of key terms. The introduction covers the historical and literary background to the *Metamorphoses*; as a second-century text written under the high empire, it is likely to be much later than any prose sixth-form students will have read before, and the introduction therefore covers key aspects of genre, literary sensibility, and intellectual and social outlook which make this text distinctively of its time.

The notes to the narrative itself aim to help students bridge the gap between GCSE and AS level Latin, and focus therefore on the harder points of grammar and word order, the rhetorical construction of Apuleius' narrative, and the differences between Classical prose and

Apuleius' later Latin. While there is mainly a linguistic bent to the notes, there is also limited reference to the structural, rhetorical, and poetic devices of which Apuleius makes use, but these are kept to a minimum. Especially in an author as conscious of sound and style as Apuleius, it is hoped that students will soon learn to spot devices and techniques themselves. At the end of the book is a full vocabulary list for all the words contained in the prescribed sections, with words in OCR's Defined Vocabulary List for AS Level Latin flagged by means of an asterisk.

There are many people without whose support this work would have not been completed, foremost amongst whom stands my wife, whose patience is truly Penelopean. I am deeply indebted to Alice Wright and her colleagues at Bloomsbury for all their help with this project. Thanks must also be expressed to the religious, royal and ancient foundation of Christ's Hospital, which, more than merely supporting my work (especially in the form of its excellent Head of Classics, Ed Hatton), nurtured two of the great English Classicists whose scholarship underpins this commentary, E.J. Kenney and Stephen Harrison. I am immensely grateful to these and many others on whose shoulders I stand, and apologize for any errors or failings, which are undoubtedly my own.

Stuart R. Thomson
Eastertide 2017

Introduction

Apuleius: The author and his context

His life and works

The eighteenth-century historian Edward Gibbon famously designated the Roman empire of the second century AD as 'the period in the history of the world, during which the condition of the human race was most happy and prosperous'. Without uncritically accepting Gibbon's judgement, it was certainly into a peaceful, prosperous North Africa under Roman rule that Apuleius was born, sometime in the 120s. In that cosmopolitan empire, he carved out a career for himself as a celebrated writer, orator, Platonic philosopher and professional intellectual.

What information we have of his life comes from his own works, and from comments by St Augustine of Hippo, a fellow North African writer clearly familiar with the writings of Apuleius several centuries later. He was born into a wealthy provincial family in a city (*colonia*) called Madauros in the province of Africa Proconsularis (now M'daurouch in modern-day Algeria), several hundred kilometres inland of Carthage (modern Tunis); his father achieved the highest political office in the *colonia* and left Apuleius and his brother a sizeable fortune at his death.

Although there had been Roman influence in this part of North Africa since the days of Massinissa, ally of the great Roman general Scipio in the Second Punic War (late third century BC), Punic culture and language (that is, the language and culture of Carthage) remained strong, and it is not unlikely that the first language Apuleius spoke was Punic, rather than Latin, as was the case with Apuleius' own stepson Pudens (*Apol.* 98), and, a generation later, the North African-born emperor, Septimius Severus.

It is Apuleius' facility with and mastery of the language of Rome which made his career, however, and his Latin literary education would have begun in Madauros, where the empire had made its language the standard for the literary and legal worlds. For more serious education he was sent to Carthage, learning grammar and rhetoric, and probably also developing a grounding in Platonic philosophy. From there his studies took him further afield, to Athens, where his studies in Greek (started in Carthage) were perfected, and then later to Rome, and there is some likelihood that he also travelled to other centres of imperial intellectual life such as Smyrna, Pergamum and Ephesus; he undoubtedly had contact with the major intellectuals and writers of his time at these hubs of culture and learning. This kind of wide educational travelling among the literary elite was not uncommon in the empire – his contemporary Aulus Gellius studied and lived in Athens, and similar educational journeys are recorded by the Greek sophist Lucian and the second-century Alexandrian Christian author Clement.

On his way back to North Africa, at Oea (modern Tripoli), Apuleius met and married a wealthy and much older widow, Prudentilla, mother of Pontianus, a fellow student he had met on his travels. The match was not as pleasing to other members of her family as it was to his friend Pontianus, and he was taken to court in 158–9, with the accusation that Prudentilla had been induced to marry him by witchcraft. His defence, which still survives, is a rhetorical *tour de force,* a speech called *Pro se de magia* ('In self-defence on a charge of magic'; more commonly called his *Apologia*); it laid the grounds for a triumphant return to Carthage, where he seems to have had a prosperous career as a speaker and writer, was elected to a priesthood, and voted a public statue. A collection of extracts from his speeches survives under the title of the *Florida,* and a number of other works of disputed authenticity (*De deo Socratis, De Platone* and *De Mundo*) suggest his development as a philosophical expositor of Greek ideas to a Roman audience.

Where in this career does the *Metamorphoses* fit, his most famous work? Nothing in the text itself gives conclusive evidence, although some scholars have seen in the exuberant fiction the creation of a young and frivolous Apuleius writing for a more cosmopolitan Roman audience. On the other hand, the themes in the *Metamorphoses* of magic and sorcery do not seem to have been brought up in accusation against him at his trial in 158–9, and further, the allusions in the work to trumped-up charges, defended by brilliant rhetoric, after which the speaker is awarded an honorific statue, and particularly apposite remarks by Venus about the suspicions aroused by a country wedding (which had formed part of the concern around Apuleius' marriage to Prudentilla), seem too similar to biographical fact to be coincidental. So sometime after his return to Carthage in the 160s or later seems the most plausible date.

The intellectual context

Although Apuleius' education and (extant) literary output was in Latin, his educational and literary outlook was fundamentally shaped by the major intellectual currents in the Greco-Roman world, in which Greek was regarded as the premier language for cultural production. More particularly, rhetorical performance in Greek by orators harking back in content, style and literary allusion to the glory days of fifth-century Greece, shaped the intellectual atmosphere of the Roman empire at this period. This efflorescence of Greek rhetoric and writing is referred to as the Second Sophistic, a term coined by Philostratus (*c.* 170–250), named after the self-conscious revival of the cultural melting-pot of classical Athens with its influx of sophists, teachers of rhetoric and philosophy. Apuleius is a contemporary of these (second) sophists – Lucian, Aelius Aristides, Dio of Prusa and those in their circles.

In broad terms, the key themes and features of this kind of literature are a concern for linguistic purity, usually in the form of almost hyper-Atticized Greek and a focus on rhetorical performance, particularly extempore epideictic rhetoric (off-the-cuff show speeches). Culturally, this literature pivots around the negotiation between Greek and Roman identity and power, with the concept of *paideia*, culture or education, as the hinge. This immensely important property was wielded like a weapon or spent like currency by the elite sophists, and traded in, on a smaller scale, by the penumbra of the *pepaideumenoi* (cultured elite) surrounding them. So, although his medium is Greek, not Latin, Apuleius has been referred to as a 'Latin Sophist' and we see reflections of the Second Sophistic throughout the extracts of the *Metamorphoses* here: deep concern for literary tradition, with complex and subtle allusions and intertextual play, a showy, performance-like use of language with a taste for archaisms, and rhetorical flourishes like ecphrases (see pp. 24–27 below, on V.22).

The *Metamorphoses*

Overview

The *Metamorphoses*, also known as *The Golden Ass,* is the most well-known of Apuleius' works. It tells the story of a wealthy, educated young man (in many respects remarkably similar to the author) called Lucius, who is introduced after an anonymous prologue promising a series of entertaining Greek tales. The novel is divided into eleven books – an unusual number for ancient literature – but the main narrative of Lucius' transformation and adventures often plays second fiddle to a series of embedded tales: some comic, some bawdy, some violent, but all entertaining.

Book I: Lucius (the narrator) tells of his journey to Thessaly; along the way he is told a tale of a man called Socrates who was murdered by magic after an affair with a witch. Lucius arrives at Hypata, his destination, and meets his host Milo.

Book II: The next day, Lucius meets and visits the house of Byrrhaena, a family friend; an ecphrasis (a literary description of an artwork; see pp. 24–27 for discussion of this feature) of a statue of Diana and Actaeon foreshadows his own bestial metamorphosis. He is warned about the magical practices of Pamphile, Milo's wife, which only arouses Lucius' curiosity (his characteristic vice). Back at Milo's house, Lucius begins to embark upon a love affair with Photis, Milo's slave-girl. At a dinner party he hears another tale of witchcraft, this time about a man called Thelyphron, who has been humiliated and maimed by the action of witches. On his way back home, the drunken Lucius is set upon by thieves, but he kills them all at Milo's door.

Book III: The following morning Lucius is arrested and charged with the murder of the three thieves; despite a passionate rhetorical defence, he is convicted and made to uncover his victims' corpses: to his astonishment, they turn out to be merely wine-skins. In his embarrassment, it is explained that the practical joke is part of the town's celebrations of the festival of laughter, and a statue is erected in his honour. (This section is usually read as based on Apuleius' own experience of the sham charge regarding his wife and his successful defence, although modulated to a comic key.) Photis confesses that she aided Pamphile in magically animating the wine-skins, and several nights later, she allows Lucius to see Pamphile turn herself into a bird; Lucius attempts to undergo the same magical transformation, but Photis, using the wrong ointment, accidentally turns him into an ass instead. She promises to cure him at dawn, but during the night, Lucius the ass is stolen by robbers.

Book IV: Lucius is taken to the robbers' cave, and we are treated to three tales of their exploits, all ending in comic failure, which they tell over dinner. The robbers go out the same night and return with a prisoner, a beautiful young girl, Charite. The robbers' housekeeper tells the tale of Cupid and Psyche to try to calm the distraught girl. This tale, from which our selection is taken, is the longest embedded tale in the *Metamorphoses*, and continues through to the middle of the sixth book: the following section of this introduction will cover it in more detail.

Book VI: At the conclusion of the tale, Lucius attempts to escape, carrying the girl with him on his back, but they are caught and the robbers plan a grim fate for the escapees.

Book VII: A stranger arrives at the robbers' cave, claiming to be the infamous bandit Haemus. He tells several tales of derring-do, and offers to become their leader; they accept, and take his advice to sell the girl rather than kill her. Lucius realizes (eventually) that Haemus is, in fact, the girl's fiancé, Tlepolemus, in disguise. Tlepolemus drugs the robbers and effects an escape with Charite carried out on Lucius' back. After the happy marriage, as a reward, Lucius is sent to their country estate – but there he is mistreated by a woman and a cruel boy. The boy is eaten by a bear, and Lucius, blamed for the misfortune, is attacked by the boy's mother, but he successfully wards her off with a stream of liquid dung.

Book VIII: A messenger brings the news that Tlepolemus has been murdered, and Charite has killed herself. The slaves, panicked at the news, run off, taking Lucius with them. Their journey is beset with disasters: they risk an attack by wolves, are chased by dogs, and have to escape a devouring serpent disguised as an old man. They sell Lucius on to a group of travelling charlatans, disreputable priests of the Syrian goddess, who make their money duping credulous and superstitious peasants. At the close of the book it looks as though the priests might slaughter Lucius to make up for a stolen joint of venison.

Book IX: Lucius escapes his fate by pretending to be rabid, and, as he travels on, hears an extremely lewd tale of a cheating wife. The priests are arrested for theft from a temple, and Lucius is again sold and put to work in a mill. Lucius hears another two bawdy tales of adultery, and then assists in revealing the adultery of the miller's wife. The miller punishes her lover in a surprising way; but the miller's wife, thrown out of the house, takes her revenge, killing the miller by witchcraft. Lucius is sold to a gardener, and then commandeered by a soldier.

Book X: Lucius is left temporarily by the soldier at a house where he hears another tale, this one of murder and medicine. Lucius is sold by the soldier to a pair of cooks, who discover him eating their food; his strange eating habits are turned into a public spectacle, and he is taught more tricks and taken to Corinth. An aristocratic lady takes her pleasure with Lucius, which encourages his owner to contemplate using him for display in the arena: to have sexual intercourse with a woman condemned for poisoning. Lucius, not enthused at this plan for a career on stage, escapes and falls asleep on a beach at Cenchreae, just outside of Corinth.

Book XI: Lucius, awaking at night on the beach, prays to the moon, who appears in the form of the goddess Isis. She instructs him that he can be cured by participating in her festival. The cure is successful; Lucius finally regains human form, and becomes an initiate and devotee of the goddess, and after a trip home, he goes to Rome to be further initiated into the mysteries of Osiris, where he ends the tale as a minor priest of the cult, financing his devotion to the Egyptian deities by his career as a lawyer.

Genre and sources

The *Metamorphoses* is the only 'novel' to survive by Apuleius, and one of the very few exemplars of this genre in Latin to survive from antiquity. I use inverted commas because the connotations that the term conveys in the present day are quite different to what we see in the ancient form which goes under the name; one of the reasons for the interpretative disagreements which mark scholarship on the *Metamorphoses* is that there are so few works which might help us as comparisons or contrasts.

While there are a small number of Greek prose works, known as the Greek novels, their swashbuckling romantic tales of lovers separated by pirates, adventures and other various trials, before inevitably they find each other and live happily ever after, read quite differently to the (very few) Roman novels. Indeed, along with the *Satyrica* of Petronius, the *Metamorphoses* is the only pre-Christian Latin prose fiction which is not a direct translation of a Greek text; in both, the setting is a realist backdrop of the Roman empire, with a mostly first-person narration containing extensive inserted tales. Despite a low-life realism, the novels are highly literary, with extensive allusion to other literary genres, and notable parody of the romantic themes of the Greek novels.

The form and content of the *Metamorphoses* was undoubtedly also influenced by a genre of stories called 'Milesian tales'; the first sentence of the work begins: *at ego tibi sermone isto Milesio varias fabulas conseram* ('but I will stitch together for you various tales in that Milesian style'). Here again we have the problem that almost none of this genre actually survives from the ancient world, although the references to it suggest that the content was ribald and comic: Ovid (*Tristia* II.413, 443–4) makes reference to the famous Greek writer of Milesian tales, Aristides of Miletus, and his Latin translator, Sisenna, in these terms. The idea of a framing narrative, into which self-contained ribald stories were stitched, and possibly the use of a first-person narrator, are elements which Apuleius took from the Milesian tales.

The framing narrative of the man turned into an ass also has a more direct literary antecedent: at the close of the prologue, we are promised a *fabulam Graecanicam* ('a Grecian tale'), and it seems that Apuleius has borrowed the key points of the narrative wholesale from a Greek original, known as the *Onos* (the Greek for ass). Whilst the Greek original doesn't survive, an epitome of the tale has come down to us falsely attributed to the sophistic author Lucian, and there is a comparison drawn up by the Byzantine patriarch Photius comparing this version to a longer version of the ass-tale, called (like Apuleius') the *Metamorphoses*, attributed to Lucius of Patrae. The character of Lucius, the framing story of the transformation into an ass, and many of the inserted tales are likely to have come from this Greek original, although scholars generally agree that the Cupid and Psyche episode (amongst other features) is an original Apuleian addition.

Apuleius' eleventh book, however, strikes quite a different note to the *Onos*; the Greek finishes with a ribald episode absent from our text, in which the human lover of Lucius-ass expresses her disappointment with his transformation back into human form, because of his now human-sized body parts. Apuleius' account of the Isiac initiation, references to mystery cults, and closure on a note of seeming joy and lasting fidelity are elements unique to his version.

Interpretations

Appropriately for a work titled for fluidity of form, the *Metamorphoses* has always confused and divided critics. It has been misread as autobiography (by no less an autobiographer than St. Augustine, at *De civitate dei* 18.18), lauded as an edifying spiritual work by its first English translator, derided as a derivative patchwork of earlier sources, and praised as a rich example of deeply ironic comedy. For the first half of the twentieth century, the literary quality of the work went underappreciated, judged as possessing no unity and little artistic value. More recent scholarship has been more positive in its assessment, emphasizing the cleverness and complexity of its literary techniques, and in particular its sophisticated narrative strategies; and secondly, the work's engagement with religious and philosophical content and symbolism has been reassessed. Many of the issues in its interpretation hinge on the relationship between book XI and the rest of the work, but also key to many of the overall interpretations has been the Cupid and Psyche episode, with its possibilities of its religious and/or philosophical interpretation.

In terms of the narrative structure, the application of seemingly complex narratological theory, at first rather overwhelming in its complexity, makes sense when the text's own concern for narrative complexity, reliability, and the role of the narrator is noted. The hugely influential work of Jack Winkler (1985) and the exhaustive commentaries of the Groningen group both use narratological theory extensively in their interpretations. This kind of theory is, in simple terms, the recognition that the framing and method of telling of stories influences how readers approach them – how the narrator (Lucius, or any of the other embedded narrators, like the old woman in the Cupid and Psyche episode) is involved in the action, whether they are trustworthy, or influenced by their later experiences in the re-telling of the story, and so on. The question becomes more complex when we consider the process of reading and the reader's partial knowledge: does our perspective on the narrative change retrospectively as we discover more about the narrator – does our realization that Lucius the narrator is now an Isiac devotee (after we have finished reading book XI) change how we re-read his retelling of his earlier adventures? Does our interpretation of the Cupid and Psyche story change when we see its themes mirrored in Lucius' own fall and redemption?

In particular, the distance between the perspective of the narrator, Lucius, and the author, Apuleius, has been often debated. Two passages have been at the heart of this debate: the prologue, and the infamous 'man from Madauros' passage in book XI. Both passages pivot around the relationship between Lucius, the narrator, and the author: thus, the unnamed speaker in the prologue has been variously identified as Lucius, Apuleius, a combination of the two, an anonymous prologue-voice, or the voice of the book itself. At XI.27, the priest Arsinius Marcellus relates to Lucius that he was expected, as a dream had warned him that 'the man from Madauros' (the home town of Apuleius, but not of Lucius) would come to him for initiation. Various solutions for the puzzling slippage have been to emend the word out of the text; as a clever *sphragis* ('seal'), or in-built acknowledgment of authorship; as a mark of the autobiographical seriousness of the Isiac initiation; or as a deliberately playful complication of the convention of the fictive first-person narrator, balancing the ambiguity of the prologue.

This is linked to the vexing question of the relationship between the eleventh book and the first ten. From the very outset, an eleventh book is unexpected: an ancient audience was used to the division of longer works into books, but generally in balanced and symmetrical ways. Epic tended to favour multiples of three (the *Iliad* and the *Odyssey* with 24, and the *Aeneid* with 12), and the Augustan poets, schemes in multiples of five (Ovid's *Metamorphoses* has fifteen, for instance); even those Greek novels favouring a different schema are at least divided into an even number of books. Thus, from the outset, Apuleius seems to have meant his eleventh book to be a surprise.

What kind of surprise is it, though? Scholars have noted the similarity between Lucius' waking on the beach at Cenchreae and praying to the rising moon and other accounts of serious personal conversion. The first fifteen chapters of book XI present the longest stretch of consistently elevated prose in the work, but this could be argued to either rule out or conversely, to highlight, irony.

The history of interpretation of the *Metamorphoses* as a serious allegorical moral tale is a surprisingly long one: starting with Fulgentius in the fifth or sixth century, and continuing into the Renaissance and even to modern readers, the whole novel has been interpreted as a cautionary moral tale. In this reading, Lucius' initiation into Isis worship provides the serious key for deeper meanings of the seeming bawdiness of the preceding eleven books. Although this might seem far-fetched, the allegorical interpretation of apparently profane subject-matter was a common tool of the Middle Platonists from whom Apuleius developed his philosophical outlook; the suggestion of hidden, secret meaning is embedded in the narrative by Lucius' own initiation into the hidden mysteries of the cult of Isis.

Several issues make this kind of reading problematic, however: while the embedded stories in the first three books, and the tale of Cupid and Psyche, can be read as part of an overall moralizing drive, it is more difficult to fit in the more loosely connected and generally more ribald tales of the last third of the novel into such a schema.

Rather than seeing his initiation into the mysteries as delivery from the disasters into which his curiosity has pitched him, it is possible to read his enthusiasm for his new cults as yet another trap which his credulity has led him into – we might question his uncritical acceptance of the new rites, his surprise when he has to undergo (and pay for) further initiations, the figure he cuts as a shaven-headed advocate in the forum (as a buffoon, in Winkler's reading). Photius, writing about the original Greek *Onos*, Apuleius' source-text, describes it as a satire on superstition and credulity: is this Apuleius' new take on the original theme? Lucius' stylistically elevated and rhetorically impassioned account of his Isiac conversion might, instead of sincere, be read as epideictic: a showing off of obscure religious knowledge in a sophistic manner, designed to entertain rather than to convert.

Lastly, increasing attention has been paid to the philosophical underpinnings of the novel; Apuleius presented himself (in his *Apologia*), and was known to both contemporaries and posterity, as a Platonic philosopher (as attested by a statue of him erected in Madauros, and the witness of St Augustine). The Cupid and Psyche tale shows clear dependence on Plato's account of the soul in the *Phaedrus* (*Metamorphoses* V.24 and *Phaedrus* 248c), and the centrality of *curiositas* connects with Platonic themes, particularly as developed by the Platonist Plutarch (with whom Lucius claims kinship at I.2) in his work *De curiositate*. Platonic texture and allusions, however, do not mean that the work is necessarily philosophical. Again, the focus might be on the entertainment of literary games, with playful readings showing off erudition, rather than serious philosophy hidden in narrative form.

The last words on the interpretation of the *Metamorphoses*, however, can be given over to Jack Winkler, universally acknowledged as the most significant and influential interpreter of the text to date: in his words (Winkler 1985: 187), the *Metamorphoses*:

> was originally written not to be a hermetically sealed monument, to be admired only from a respectful distance, but as an open text, one that encourages participation – real embarrassment, puzzlement, disgust, laughter, tentative closures of meaning and surprising entrapments, mental rewriting ('Oh, he must mean . . '), and physical rewriting.

The tale of Cupid and Psyche

Overview and structure

The tale of Cupid and Psyche is the longest of the embedded narratives in the *Metamorphoses*, and is almost certainly an Apuleian addition. It is the only tale which takes place outside the recognizable everyday world of the Roman empire, and we are taken instead to a mythical, idealized Greek world. It sits within the overarching narrative as a story told by the robbers' housekeeper, attempting to calm the grief of the kidnapped Charite, stolen away at the very point of her marriage. The whole tale can be summarized as follows.

Psyche (Greek for 'soul') is a princess so beautiful she is worshipped by the people as an earthly Venus (IV.28); jealous, the goddess herself orders her son Cupid ('Desire') to punish Psyche (IV.30–1). Despite her beauty, therefore, she is admired but never loved, and her parents, in despair, send to an oracle, where they are given the answer that she must be exposed on a mountain top, where she will be taken in marriage by a monster (IV.33–4). She is duly left on the mountain, but rather than the expected awful fate, she is conveyed by Zephyr (the personified god of the west wind) to a magnificent palace where she is waited on by invisible attendants (IV.35–5.3). An equally invisible bridegroom comes to her at night (V.3–4). Against the advice of her unseen lover, she invites her sisters to visit her, where their jealousy is excited by her good fortune (V.5–11). They attempt to convince her that her husband is actually a serpent, who intends to devour her, and urge her to kill him to protect herself (V.12–20).

Psyche, gullible (but also culpably curious), is convinced, and dagger and lamp in hand discovers her husband is not a serpent, but the incomparably handsome Cupid (V.21–2). A drop of oil from the lamp awakens (and wounds) him, and he flees, despite the fact that Psyche is now pregnant with his child. Psyche unsuccessfully tries to kill herself (V.24–5); she takes her vengeance on her sisters, who die by throwing themselves from a cliff, convinced that Cupid is going to take them on as his lover (V.26–7). Venus, taking the role of a scorned mother-in-law, now persecutes Psyche (V.28–6.10), setting her impossible tasks, which Psyche manages to complete with the help of other creatures (VI.10–15), and the final task, a descent to the underworld, she accomplishes with supernatural aid (VI.16–20). At the final moment, however, carrying back a casket from Proserpina to Venus, she again succumbs to her vice of curiosity and opens its lid (VI.21). By this time, Cupid has recovered from his wound and escaped the watch of his mother; he finds Psyche, restores the casket to Proserpina, and pleads for his love at the throne of Jupiter (VI.22). Venus is reconciled with Psyche, and the tale ends with a happy wedding feast amongst the gods, capped by the birth of a daughter to Cupid and Psyche, Voluptas ('Pleasure', VI.23–4).

Several attempts have been made to identify the internal structure of the tale; the fact that no one system has gained general acceptance suggests that there is no clear and obvious way of understanding its design. Given that the book divisions are Apuleius' own, the tripartite structure based around them suggested by Zimmerman *et al.* (2004) is perhaps the most plausible:

A (IV.28–35): Introduction of the main characters, and the problems which lead to the drama of the tale.

B (V) Rise and fall of Psyche: her awakening as Cupid's lover, and her fall due to over-curiosity.

C (VI.1–24) Trials of Psyche, leading to her reunion with Cupid.

Within this broader understanding, there are clear structural features within the tale; a key feature is the inclusion of ecphrases (artistic descriptive scenes; see pp. 24–27 below) at four pivotal points in the tale. The first, at IV.31, describes Venus' departure to the sea: the splendour of her retinue contrast with the loneliness of Psyche. The second occurs at the opening of book V, where Cupid's palace is explored by Psyche. The ecphrasis dramatizes the fact that Psyche has entered an entirely new world, and the gloomy end of book IV is reversed by the discovery of this wonderland. The third ecphrasis is Psyche's discovery of the beauty of Cupid at V.22, the pivotal point of Psyche's fall. Lastly, a fourth ecphrasis (VI.6) returns us to Venus, describing her ascent to Olympus. The overall structure is chiastic: Venus' two different retinues, one of the sea and one of the sky, bookend two descriptions of wonder, seen through Psyche's eyes. There are two more, minor ecphrases in the trials of Psyche which parallel each other: at VI.13, Venus gives an ecphrasis of the location of Psyche's third task, and then at VI.14 we see it focalized through Psyche's eyes. These descriptive scenes serve to give colour and charm to the tale, as well as provide it with structural balance and coherence.

The story-within-a-story

Although the tale stands up perfectly well when removed from its surrounds, and has often been edited or translated as a stand-alone story, it has been carefully embedded within the larger narrative, and in many interpretations provides the key, or at least a significant piece of the puzzle, for an overarching interpretation of the novel as a whole. Walsh, in a much-quoted observation, notes that Apuleius 'has here adopted the Alexandrian technique exploited by Callimachus in his *Hecale* and taken over by Catullus in his sixty-fourth poem; *Cupid and Psyche* is a story within a story, and designed to illuminate the larger whole' (Walsh 1970: 190).

Embedding the tale across three books (a technique characteristic of Ovid in his *Metamorphoses*) secures and embeds it integrally within the work as a whole; moreover, the introduction of the tale by the old woman, *sed ego te narrationibus lepidis anilibusque fabulis protinus avocabo* ('But come, now let me take your mind off your troubles: here's a pretty fairy tale, an old woman's story'), clearly echoes the prologue of the *Metamorphoses: At ego tibi sermone isto Milesio varias fabulas conseram auresque tuas benivolas lepido susurro permulceam* ('Now what I propose in this Milesian discourse is to string together for you a series of different stories and to charm your ears, kind reader, with amusing gossip'; Kenney's translation).

The analogy between the two stories is complex: Lucius, as a hearer of the Cupid and Psyche tale, does not realize its relevance and parallelism to his own situation until his salvation by Isis; equally, the reader of the *Metamorphoses* will not realize that there might be instruction beneath the 'amusing gossip' until that same point in Lucius' retelling, his narration of his Isiac conversion.

The fable recapitulates the core elements of the story of Lucius: his transformation into an ass is the result, like Psyche's troubles, of inordinate curiosity, and his transformation back into human form takes place after a series of misfortunes which echo Psyche's trials. Resolution comes as a result of divine intervention, and Psyche's journey to the Underworld and opening of a secret casket echo elements of the Eleusinian mysteries and thus prefigure Lucius' mystic initiations into the Isis and Osiris cults in book XI. The central positioning of the tale within the *Metamorphoses* is significant: the tale itself sits in the middle of the first ten books, but Psyche's *katabasis*, her descent to the underworld, is the centre of the whole work. This is partly a reference to the centrality of similar *katabaseis* in Homer's *Odyssey* and Virgil's *Aeneid*, it also points forwards to Lucius' own *katabasis* in book XI, after which he is united to Isis, as Psyche is joined to Cupid.

On another level, the tale fits into a carefully interwoven complex of narratives and themes which binds together the disparate elements and characters of IV.23–VIII.14. The so-called 'Charite-complex', identified by Carl Schlam (see further reading), integrates three strands of the narrative in a delicate counterpoint: Charite and Tlepolemus, Cupid and Psyche, and the story of Lucius himself. The Cupid and Psyche tale echoes Charite's own interrupted wedding, and prefigures her eventual liberation and successful marriage (though without the subsequent reversal of fortune that befalls both Lucius and Charite). Narratologically, the balance between the Charite's back-story (told by Charite herself to the old woman) and the tale of Cupid and Psyche (told by the old woman to Charite), rests on a series of opposites: narrator and audience swap places, from opposite perspectives; young/old, rich/poor, real-life tragedy/mythic happily-ever-after fairytale. As a binding recurrent theme, a series of clever deceits tie the stories together: Psyche is deceived by her sisters, but in turn causes their deaths by a clever deceit of her own; Tlepolemus deceives the robbers by an Odyssean trick (getting them drunk), but is himself later undone, deceived by a rival, who himself, tricked by drugged wine, is exposed by Charite before her death.

The sources of the tale

While the tale is an Apuleian insertion into the Greek *Onos*, it is clearly not just an imaginative tour-de-force of the author's creative powers; elements of the story clearly have predecessors, models and sources in earlier variants. Accounts of the tale (especially in the first half of the twentieth century) have attempted to find an exclusive source in folktale, myth or literature.

Certainly, the overall narrative seems to have connections with folklore: at the very beginning of modern research into folk traditions, the brothers Grimm noted the folkloric elements of Apuleius' tale, and with the technical development of what is called the Finnish historical-geographical method, hundreds of parallel folk-stories could be found for Cupid and Psyche. Core motifs are the search for a lost husband, who initially appears as an animal or monster, and whose loss follows the violation of a taboo, and the fulfillment of impossible tasks set by a witch.

What is lacking from this account, however, is the importance of the figures of Cupid and Psyche themselves: the folklore parallels give us tales of anonymous or at least generic husbands and wives, rather than the Soul and Love personified, and while many motifs and elements are shared, the narrative as a whole is largely unparalleled. More serious criticisms have been levelled at the attempted scientific nature of folklore research in general, critiquing the attempts to look for origins for particular tale-types in some pure, non-elite, non-literary, historically unbroken oral tradition. In the most strident objection, folklore is itself a literary genre created in the sixteenth to eighteenth centuries, developed by writers drawing on written material of the Middle Ages and antiquity: in this view, traces of Cupid and Psyche in fairytales are just as likely to be dependent on the Apuleian tale as they are evidence for a pre-existing oral source.

Looking towards myth rather than folklore, suggestions that Apuleius was drawing on an earlier source are supported by the iconographic tradition of Cupid-and-Psyche as a pair, a representation which was popular from the sixth century BC onwards. When the oracle warns Psyche's parents of her monstrous lover as 'a creature of no mortal stock, but a cruel, wild, and fiery evil, who, flying above the sky, wearies all things, and cripples each with flame and iron, before whom Jupiter himself trembles' (*Met*. IV.33; trans. in Schlam 1992), the mystery of her lover is only conventional: this imagery of Eros/ Cupid is familiar both from literature and from art, and even expected after the introduction of our heroine as Psyche (at IV.30).

The iconography with which the audience would have been familiar depicted both Cupid and Psyche as winged creatures, part of a tradition which saw the soul figured as a butterfly, suggestive of the life of the soul after death. Often the relationship between the two characters represented Eros as a *daemon* who draws the soul towards the divine, and the embracing pair became 'an enduring expression of the goal of reunion with the divine within man with God' (Schlam 1992: 91). These representations were particularly common as funereal motifs on sarcophagi at the time of the *Metamorphoses'* composition, as an emblem of the survival or salvation of the soul after death, and this theme clearly links into Isiac interpretations of the tale. But while this iconography is certainly part of what Apuleius is playing with, these images do not seem to have been attached to a particular narrative, certainly not one as complex as the tale we have here.

Over the top of whatever elements Apuleius has taken from myth or folklore are much more literary elements: foremost, the Platonic tradition of philosophical myth-making, but more playfully, borrowing elements from genres as diverse as epic, satire, and in particular, Alexandrian poetry. The literary texture is just as much part of Apuleius' tale as any of the putative sources for it: thus Venus' opening speech (IV.30) is reminiscent of Lucretian style, but is deliberately playing on Virgil's Juno, particularly her first speech at

Aeneid I.34–49, already parodied by Ovid in his *Metamorphoses* (III.262–72). The sisters' description of the snake is another Virgilian pastiche (see notes on V.26, and below); the most extended play with the *Aeneid* is in Psyche's *katabasis,* which is 'virtually a mosaic of Virgilian phrases' (Walsh 1970: 57). This kind of intellectual game-playing is part of the competitive literary culture which formed Apuleius' cultural backdrop, and while an audience does not need to recognize an intertextual allusion to understand the story, often it adds an extra level of characterization, emotion or wit to the narrative.

The meaning(s) of the tale

There have been readings of the tale which see in it quite specific Isiac resonances, and incorporate the tale into an overall interpretation of the work as serious Isiac propaganda: a 1953 article by a German scholar, Reinhold Merkelbach, stands at the head of this tradition ('Eros und Psyche', *Philologus* 102 (1953): 103–16). Although his reading is not the mainstream one, it still has adherents in more recent scholarship. Merkelbach notes that Isis has both transcendent and narrative mythic forms: the former as the personified hand of fortune, and the latter as the itinerant goddess, searching for the dismembered parts of Osiris; thus, the heavenly Venus represents the first aspect, and the wandering Psyche the second.

More influential and convincing a reading, however, is based on the known philosophical leanings of Apuleius. It is the tale of Cupid and Psyche more than any other part of the *Metamorphoses* which has given rise to Platonic readings of the work. Kenney (1990) has noted the influence of the discussion of love in Plato's *Symposium*: in this work, Venus and Eros (i.e. Cupid) are discussed as each having a heavenly and an earthly form (Venus Urania and Venus Pandemos, with Erotes to match): one for the love of souls, the other for love of bodies (180d–181b). Apuleius himself paraphrased the work in his *Apologia* (12), and the argument runs that the fable dramatizes the conflict between earthly Venus and heavenly Eros, and thus is an allegory of the competition between, and the victory of, spiritual love (the love of virtue) over physical lust. Mark Edwards ('The Tale of Cupid and Psyche', *ZPE* 94 (1992): 77–94) gives a detailed account of parallels to Apuleius' story in Neo-Platonist, Gnostic and eastern mythic traditions, and shows how such complex allegorical story-telling was part and parcel of the spiritual and intellectual milieu of the second century. Even if we do not read the tale as straightforward, serious, philosophical mythic allegory, therefore, it seems more than likely that Apuleius deliberately plays with features of this kind of writing. As so often in the *Metamorphoses,* whether Apuleius is sermonizing or jesting is difficult to tell.

Apuleius' style

General stylistic features

It can never be far from the reader's mind that Apuleius was trained and practised as an orator and professional rhetorician. His writing is constructed with an ear for its effect when read aloud, for the delight in the sounds and the images created by them: it strikes the reader as exuberant, over-the-top, showy, and intricate. It used to be common to refer to Latin of the first century BC as 'golden' and that of the first century AD as 'silver' (being inferior); and, following this pattern, it was a common literary judgment to see both Latin and Greek literature of the later empire as degenerate, derivative and second-rate. More recently, however, critical scholarship has been more positive in its assessment, underscoring the creativity, playfulness, and complexity of imperial literature; Apuleius has benefitted from a serious reconsideration of his literary value during the last few decades.

The key features of Apuleius' language are 'exuberance and richness' (Kenney 1990a: 29): you will notice that reading and translating Apuleius is quite a different experience to reading and translating Caesar, Cicero, Tacitus, or the other prose authors you may have studied up to this point. With Apuleius, it is worthwhile, once you have got over the initial hurdle of unpicking the syntax and vocabulary, to go back over the sentence, paragraph or passage (whether it be a speech, narrative description, or other set-piece) and read it out aloud. The characteristic features of Apuleius you might be able to spot occur on a number of levels within the text:

- Vocabulary: hugely varied, with frequent poetic usages, archaisms, neologisms (often formed from poetic or archaic forms), or words used in unfamiliar or unusual senses, and diminutives.
- Sentence structure: tends to be paratactic rather than hypotactic; that is, independent clauses (often balanced in contrast or parallelism) rather than strings of subordinate clauses. Apuleius is also much given to different kinds of repetition: pleonasm, variation and amplification. In both of these habits, Apuleius should be more reader- and translator-friendly than many classical authors (like Cicero, Livy or Tacitus, all of whom tend to more complex periodic construction).
- Attention to sound: Apuleius frequently uses alliteration and assonance to adorn his sentences. Importantly, he is also one of most attentive authors to prose rhythm – the use of metrical formulae (like you may be familiar with in poetry), particularly to mark the conclusion of sentences (called *clausulae*).
- Topoi (literary commonplaces): you will find a large number of set rhetorical pieces; often these are straightforwardly in the form of formal speeches, but also, for example, in ornate descriptive passages (ecphrases).

- Allusion and intertextuality: Apuleius is often consciously and deliberately playing with a rich literary tradition. An audience does not need to be highly-educated and intimately familiar with the Latin literary tradition to appreciate the *Metamorphoses*, but without such knowledge they will miss a large number of jokes, ironies, wry comparisons, and general literary play.

Prose-rhythm

From at least the classical period, Roman authors were clearly conscious of the aural effect created by patterns of heavy and light syllables in formal spoken prose. Cicero records that a particularly apt rhythm could bring about spontaneous applause (*Or.* 214), and his use of different rhythmical patterns set the standard for later authors. Part of this tradition is based on Greek models and theories of prose-rhythm, but Latin developed its distinctive tradition and style. In particular, the ends of sentences, called *clausulae,* were the focus for judicious use of sonorous patterns; partly for purely aesthetic reasons, but undoubtedly also for practical purposes: in a tradition where literature was still fundamentally meant to be read aloud, but in which scribal convention did not often show sense divisions in sentences, or even divisions between words, rhythmical markers for the ends of periods or cola (natural sense breaks within sentences) were useful in complex sentences.

It is important to note that the patterns are quantitative, rather than (as is common in English poetry or prose) stress-based – i.e. they are based on length of syllables (heavy or light, marked – and ∪ respectively, or x where a syllable can be long or short), rather than emphasized syllables within words; so neither word-accent nor word-division make a difference to the use of these rhythms. As in verse, elision is taken into account: a vowel ending a word, if followed by one starting with a vowel, is not pronounced – so *totisque illis* in the first section from the set text would have been pronounced *totisqu~illis* with four syllables.

The basic clausula patterns preferred by Cicero are the ditrochee (– ∪ – x), especially with a preceding cretic (– ∪ – | – ∪ – x), the double cretic (– ∪ – | – ∪ x), and the cretic followed by either a trochee or a spondee (– ∪ – | – x). These patterns can also be varied by resolution – the replacement of a long syllable by two short syllables. The pattern of *ēssĕ vĭdĕātŭr* (a resolved version of the third form above) even became such a trademark of Cicero's that later writers avoided it unless deliberately trying to evoke Cicero.

Apuleius, as a rhetorician, and as an author distinctly conscious of his literary heritage, is remarkably consistent in his usage of these *clausulae*: depending on the method of counting used, up to 92.5 per cent of Apuleius' sentences end in a recognized rhythm; another analysis suggests that Apuleius follows Ciceronian principles just under 70 per cent of the time (Kenney 1990a: 31). A sense of prose-rhythm is clearly also present in the careful manipulation of the lengths of clauses (in terms of number of syllables); clauses can build to a climax with ascending numbers of syllables, or be balanced in equal lengths; the best example in the current selection is in V.21: *festinat, differt; audet, trepidat; diffidit, irascitur* (see note in commentary). Whilst prose-rhythm analysis doesn't often tend to make for the same examination-ready commentary notes as other rhetorical features, it is important nonetheless to keep in mind that throughout the composition of the *Metamorphoses,* the aural effect of the prose was consistently one of Apuleius' fundamental considerations.

Ecphrasis: Cupid's beauty (V.22)

Particular instances of the stylistic elements already discussed are picked out in the commentary, but it is worth examining in detail a few passages from the selection which are particularly indicative of the concerns of the sophistic style in which Apuleius writes, and which exemplify his own mastery of these techniques.

Ecphrasis (sometimes written *ekphrasis*) is the vivid literary depiction of a work of art, developed as a set-piece designed to show off rhetorical skill. At the root of the tradition is the lengthy, detailed description of Achilles' shield in *Iliad* XVIII, famously echoed by Virgil in his description of Aeneas' shield in *Aeneid* VIII. The technique reached the peak of its popularity amongst the authors of the Second Sophistic, when whole works were comprised solely of ecphrases of fictional artworks.

As we noted above on the structure of the tale of Cupid and Psyche, four key ecphrases mark out significant turning points in the tale, including one in the selection covered by this commentary, the description of the sleeping Cupid at V.22: 'the living god is treated as a work of art' (Kenney 1990 *ad loc.*). The ecphrasis is introduced by the illumination of Psyche's lamp:

> Sed cum primum luminis oblatione tori secreta claruerunt, videt omnium ferarum mitissimam dulcissimamque bestiam, *ipsum illum Cupidinem* formonsum deum formonse cubantem, cuius aspectu lucernae quoque lumen hilaratum increbruit et acuminis sacrilegi novaculam paenitebat.

> But as soon as the lamp was raised on high, the mysteries of her bed shone forth: she saw the gentlest and sweetest of all wild creatures, that very Cupid himself, a beautiful god beautifully lying. At his appearance the cheerful light of the lamp burned higher [or the lamp's eyes lit up cheerfully] and the dagger repented its sacrilegious edge.
>
> (Trans. Tatum 1979: 152, lightly adapted)

The use of vocabulary is typically Apuleian; *oblatio* is a technical legal term for presenting evidence or offering bail, and is introduced into literary prose by Apuleius. The adjective *formo(n)sus* is very rare: attested only before the *Metamorphoses* in a poem by Propertius

(II.3.17) and in the technical writer Quintilian (*Inst. Or.* VIII.3.10). It is possible that Apuleius is deliberately playing with this reference to Propertius, who uses the word in describing the beauty of Cynthia, a passage which bears other similarities to this one. The clever use of *lumen* in both its literal sense of 'light' but also in the poetic sense to stand for 'eye' underscores the personification of the lamp. This personification looks forward to the apostrophe of V.23, and adds vividness to the scene, in which light, colour and the visual are central.

Most notable in reading the passage, however, is the overwhelming alliteration of liquid consonants (*l, m, n, r*) at the beginning, shifting to *c* and *t* sounds in the second half of the sentence, along with the assonance of *i* and *u*. The sounds echo and draw attention to the object in the middle of the sentence, *ipsum illum Cupidinem*, the first time Psyche's lover is explicitly identified in the text (although the astute reader should already have guessed). Further considering the effect on the ear, the sentence finishes on one of the most recognizably Cicerion *clausulae*, a ditrochee (– ∪ – x) with a preceding cretic (– ∪ –): *novāculūm pnītēbāt*.

The oxymoronic juxtaposition of *omnium ferarum mitissimam dulcissimamque bestiam*, underscored by the double superlatives, emphasizes her surprise, but also plays with the literary tradition of Cupid and the epithets which he was often given in poetry. The polyptoton of *formonsum deum formonse cubantem* is striking, particularly as *formo(n)sus* is a very rare word before Apuleius. This kind of repetition is common in Latin poetry, especially Virgil and Lucretius, but also owes something to Greek literary background, especially over-the-top 'Gorgianic' rhetoric (named after Gorgias of Leontini, famous for privileging style over substance). The literary allusions go further, however, and there is likely a Homeric play here: the echo of a recurring phrase, κεῖτο μέγας μεγαλωστί ('he lay great in his greatness', *Il.* 16.776, 18.26–7, *Od.* 24.39–40) lends epic awe to the scene.

The ecphrasis proper which follows is marked out (as also the one at V.1) with the leading verb *videt*, and accords with typical rhetorical practice by starting at Cupid's head and working downwards:

> Videt capitis aurei genialem caesariem ambrosia temulentam, cervices lacteas genasque purpureas pererrantes crinium globos decoriter impeditos, alios antependulos, alios retropendulos, quorum splendore nimio fulgurante iam et ipsum lumen lucernae vacillabat; per umeros volatilis dei pinnae roscidae micanti flore candicant et quamvis alis quiescentibus extimae plumulae tenellae ac delicatae tremule resultantes inquieta lasciviunt.

> She saw a rich head of golden hair dripping with ambrosia, a milk-white neck, and rosy cheeks over which there strayed coils of hair becomingly arranged, some hanging in front, some behind, shining with such extreme brilliance that the lamplight itself flickered uncertainly. On the shoulders of the flying god there sparkled wings, dewy-white with glistening sheen, and though they were at rest the soft delicate down at their edges quivered and rippled in incessant play.
>
> (Trans. Kenney 2004)

The emphasis on words of light and colour is clear; with *decoriter impeditos* we get a sense of artful disorder; the vocabulary is full of Apuleian coinages: both *antependulos* and *retropendulos*, for instance. The last sentence quoted here (the ecphrasis continues for a few lines more) is replete with sensuous alliteration of *l*, especially in the diminutives *plumulae tenellae*. The overall effect of the ecphrasis is the representation of a luminous image into equally luminous prose: the visual is echoed and translated into the aural.

Intertextuality: Psyche's sisters (V.17–20)

The complexity of Apuleius' relationship with the Latin literary canon can be illustrated by the way Psyche's relationship with her sisters is woven throughout with literary allusions. When Psyche is hesitating whether to attack her lover (V.21), she recalls heroines from Ovid; the military language of the sisters reminds us of Caesar; the sisters' threats about being buried in a beast seem Lucretian. But it is the subtle and recurring connections between Psyche's sisters and Virgil's *Aeneid*, especially its account of the fall of Troy in Book II, which contribute the most to the overall characterization of the relationship. The different layers of intertextuality are overlapping, sometimes crystal clear, sometimes speculative; some resonances might be accidental, or deliberate only insofar as they show off how well-read Apuleius is, but many are clearly meant to recall the source-text and add extra depth to the scene or the character.

When the sisters first try to convince Psyche that her husband is in fact a monster, their speech is introduced with an indication of their falsehood: *lacrimisque pressura palpebrum coactis* ('with tears forced by rubbing their eyelids'). These 'forced tears' recall *Aeneid* II.195–6: *talibus insidiis periurique arte Sinonis | credita res, captique dolis lacrimisque coactis* ('with such a snare and the oath-breaking art of Sinon the thing was believed, and we were captured by his trickery and forced tears'), where Sinon, the Greek liar, tricks the Trojans into accepting the famous Trojan horse and thus bringing about their own downfall. This is the only other place in Latin literature where the phrase *lacrimis coactis* carries the same meaning; Apuleius has tricked out the phrase more fulsomely with the typically alliterative *pressura palpebrum*, but the underlying themes of deceptiveness gives a sense of epic scale to Psyche's foreshadowed disaster.

The (fictional) serpent which the sisters go on to describe is almost a Virgilian pastiche (e.g. *Aeneid* II.381, *Georgics* III.421 and 430–1, and IV.458) but echoes most closely the description of the snake which kill Laocoön and his two sons in *Aeneid* II (ll. 206ff). These snakes and the death of Laocoön are interpreted as an omen that the Trojan horse should be received into the city; Laocoön had warned against it and even struck the horse – but of course, it is a deliberate false omen, designed to trap the Trojans. In the same way, the sister's advice is deliberately deceptive.

Lastly, when the sisters overcome Psyche's resistance to their scheme, their victory is figured in language reminiscent of the Greeks taking Troy:

> tunc nanctae iam *portis patentibus* nudatum sororis animum facinerosae mulieres, omissis tectae machinae latibulis, destrictis gladiis fraudium simplicis puellae paventes cogitationes *invadunt*.

> (*Met.* V.19)

At the moment when these wicked women have occupied their sister's mind, defenceless, its gates thrown open, with their covered siege engine left behind, swords of treachery unsheathed, they invade the fearful thoughts of the guileless girl.

> *invadunt* urbem somno vinoque sepultam;
> caeduntur vigiles, *portisque patentibus* omnis
> accipiunt socios atque agmina conscia iungunt.

> (*Aeneid* II.265–7)

They invade the city buried in sleep and wine, and the guards are cut down, and with the gates thrown open they let in all their comrades and join together their ranks as accomplices.

In addition to the verbal resonances picked out here, the phrase *tectae machinae latibulis* picks up the Trojan horse, referred to as a *machina* several times in the *Aeneid* (II.46, 151 and 237), and as *latebrae* twice, at II.38, 55. (The seriousness of the situation is possibly picked up by the heavily spondaic clausula, a cretic + dispondee: *cogitātiōn|ēs īnvādūnt*. This kind of interpretation of clausulae is notoriously fickle, however!)

Thus we see, over several chapters of the *Metamorphoses,* a careful parallel built up, encouraging the audience through specific verbal references to equate the sisters with the treacherous Greeks of Virgil's *Aeneid*; the intertext serves to foreshadow the action as well as characterize the sisters as underhanded, deceptive, and ultimately desctructive.

Glossary of stylistic terms

alliteration: repetition of consonant sounds.

anaphora: repetition of a word, especially at the beginning of successive clauses.

apostrophe: breaking out from narration to make a direct address.

asyndeton: lack of connective particles between clauses.

assonance: repetition of vowel sounds.

bathos: an effect of anticlimax, by dropping from elevated speech to colloquial or ridiculous.

chiasmus: inverted parallelism – i.e. any arrangement of words in a pattern of A-B-B-A (e.g. by part of speech, by case, by sound).

diminutive: a form of a noun denoting that it is a small or immature version; like the English 'booklet' or 'piglet' for small forms of book and pig.

homoioteleuton: similar endings, giving the effect of rhyme.

hypallage: transferring an element from what it agrees with in sense to another part of the sentence; also referred to as a transferred epithet. E.g the final verse of *Adeste fideles* reads: 'Yea, Lord, we greet thee, born this happy morning' – in sense, we are happy, rather than the morning.

hyperbaton: an inversion of the normal order of words, usually for emphasis.

hypotaxis: construction of periodic sentences using subordinate clauses.

isocolon: a succession of sentences or phrases of equal length.

juxtaposition: the placing of contrasting words or ideas next to each other.

makarismos: a topos, common in ancient religious contexts, of declaring someone or something blessed: the most well-known example being the 'beatitudes' from the Sermon on the Mount, with its list of 'blessed are ...'

neologism: a newly-invented word.

onomatopoeia: words which make the sound they describe, like 'whirr' or 'buzz'.

oxymoron: a seeming contradiction in terms; literally 'sharp-dull' in Greek. E.g. *festina lente*, 'hasten slowly'.

parataxis: constructing sentences by parallel clauses, rather than by subordination.

paronomasia: play on words, punning.

pleonasm: the use of more words than are necessary, usually for emphasis.

polyptoton: repetition of a word in multiple grammatical forms.

tetracolon: a series of four parallel clauses.

topos: a traditional or formulaic theme or element in literature.

tricolon: a combination of three parallel clauses, often building up to a significant, emphasized third element.

zeugma: Also known as *syllepsis*; where a single word or phrase is used with two other parts of a sentence, but must be understood differently in relation to each. The Flanders and Swan music-hall song 'Have Some Madeira, M'Dear' is an education in zeugma; for example, 'by raising her glass, her courage, her eyes, and his hopes'.

The text

The text of the *Metamorphoses* depends on a single source, an eleventh-century manuscript held at Florence, catalogued as Laurentianus 68.2, known as F; all other extant copies derive from this single survival, although some copies were clearly made when F when was in a better condition than it is now, and where wear and tear have defaced the reading, we can often supply the deficiency from these copies. Emendations to the text have therefore been made by editors on the basis of difficulties with the Latin rather than conflicting witnesses. I have not provided an *apparatus criticus* with this text, as being unnecessary for the purposes of a school text, but I have generally followed the text printed by Purser (1913; easily available at www.thelatinlibrary.com), with some adaptations on the basis of comment either in Kenney (1990a) or Zimmerman *et al.* (2004).

Further reading

I will attempt to give here a (necessarily rather subjective) selection of the texts which would be most useful for a teacher preparing the text to consult, and which a particularly interested and capable student might be directed towards for extension. Full bibliographical references are given at the end. The most important further reading is to read the rest of the tale of Cupid and Psyche in translation, and ideally the whole of the *Metamorphoses*. There are several readily available good translations: the Penguin Classics version, Kenney (2004), is lively and readable, with an excellent brief introduction. The Loeb edition, with facing English and Latin, Hanson (1989), in two volumes, and the Oxford World Classics edition, Walsh (1994), are both also eminently accessible without sacrificing accuracy.

There are two excellent modern commentaries on Cupid and Psyche: the Cambridge 'green and yellow' commentary (although oddly not actually green and yellow, in this case) Kenney (1990a), has an extensive introduction (a fuller version than that in his Penguin translation), and brief but very useful notes. The magisterial volume on the tale of Cupid and Psyche in the Groningen Commentaries on Apuleius, by Zimmerman *et al.* (2004) is exhaustive in its treatment, including an English translation. Its cost, however, is prohibitive, unless you have access to a university library, and its depth is well beyond that needed even at undergraduate level. Surprisingly useful still is Purser's 1910 commentary, available in reprint, which gives more help than Kenney at the appropriate level for sixth-form students.

For more general reading on Apuleius, Harrison (2000) provides an excellent overview and sets the *Metamorphoses* within the context of Apuleius' wider oeuvre and his intellectual context. A broader outlook on Antonine literature, including a chapter by Kenney on Cupid and Psyche, is given by Russell (1990). The best single-volume studies on the *Metamorphoses* are Tatum (1979), Schlam (1992), both highly readable and accessible texts, and most influentially (though a more challenging read), Winkler (1985). For those interested in the literary allusiveness of Apuleius, Finkelpearl (1998) is outstanding. Walsh (1970) is useful for placing the *Metamorphoses*, and its genre as a novel, in the context of Roman literature more broadly.

Lastly, one area left untouched by this introduction has been the rich afterlife of the *Metamorphoses*, and the Cupid and Psyche episode in particular, in later literature and art. The field of classical reception is one growing in importance and visibility in the world of academic Classics, but quite apart from that, the story of later receptions of Apuleius is a fascinating one, with some particular interesting by-ways to tread, especially for those interested in Renaissance literature or art. There are two books from the last decade or so which provide excellent coverage of the field, Carver (2007) and Gaisser (2008); the overview of Cupid and Psyche in renaissance art in De Jong (1998) is also well worth perusing.

Carver, R.H.F. 2007. *The Protean Ass: The Metamorphoses of Apuleius from Antiquity to the Renaissance*. Oxford Classical Monographs. Oxford: Oxford University Press.

De Jong, J.L. 1998. "'Il Pittore a le Volte è pure Poeta": Cupid and Psyche in Italian Renaissance Painting', in M. Zimmerman, V. Hunink, *et al.* (eds.), *Aspects of Apuleius' Golden Ass. Volume II: Cupid and Psyche*. Groningen: Egbert Forsten, 189–216.

Finkelpearl, E.D. 1998. *Metamorphosis of Language in Apuleius: A Study of Allusion in the Novel*. Ann Arbor: University of Michigan Press.

Gaisser, J.H. 2008. *The Fortunes of Apuleius and the Golden Ass: A Study in Transmission and Reception*. Martin Classical Lectures. Princeton: Princeton University Press.

Hanson, J.A. (ed. and trans.) 1989. *Apuleius: Metamorphoses*. 2 Vols. Loeb Classical Library. Cambridge, MA; London: Harvard University Press.

Harrison, S.J. 2000. *Apuleius: A Latin Sophist*. Oxford: Oxford University Press.

Kenney, E.J. 1990. *Cupid and Psyche*. Cambridge: Cambridge University Press.

Kenney, E.J. 2004. *Apuleius: The Golden Ass*. Introduction and translation. Revised ed.; first published 1998. London: Penguin.

Purser, L.C. 1910. *The Story of Cupid and Psyche: as related by Apuleius*. Edited, with introduction and notes. London: George Bell.

Purser, L.C. 1913. *Apulei Psyche et Cupido*. Scriptorum classicorum bibliotheca Riccardiana. London: Lee Warner.

Russell, D.A. (ed.) 1990. *Antonine Literature*. Oxford: Oxford University Press.

Schlam, C.C. 1992. *The* Metamorphoses *of Apuleius: On Making an Ass of Oneself*. London: Duckworth.

Tatum, J. 1979. *Apuleius and* The Golden Ass. Ithaca and London: Cornell University Press.

Walsh, P.G. 1970. *The Roman Novel*. Cambridge: Cambridge University Press.

Walsh, P.G. 1994. *The Golden Ass*. Translation and introduction. Oxford: Clarendon.

Winkler, J.J. 1985. *Auctor and Actor: A Narratological Reading of Apuleius's Golden Ass*. Berkeley; Los Angeles; London: University of California Press.

Zimmerman, M., S. Panayotakis *et al.* 2004. *Apuleius Madaurensis. Metamorphoses, Book IV 28–35, V and VI 1–24. The Tale of Cupid and Psyche*. Text, Introduction and Commentary. Groningen Commentaries on Apuleius. Groningen: Egbert Forsten.

Text

The extract begins after Psyche has already been carried off by Zephyr to the mysterious palace where she is waited on by invisible attendants, and an unseen lover comes to her at night. Against his advice, she invites her sisters to visit; their jealousy excited by Psyche's good fortune, they agree to contrive her downfall.

11. placet pro bono duabus malis malum consilium, totisque illis tam pretiosis muneribus absconditis, comam trahentes et proinde ut merebantur ora lacerantes simulatos redintegrant fletus. ac sic parentes quoque redulcerato prorsum dolore raptim deserentes, vesania turgidae domus suas contendunt dolum scelestum, immo vero parricidium struentes contra sororem insontem.

interea Psychen maritus ille quem nescit rursum suis illis nocturnis sermonibus sic commonet: 'videsne quantum tibi periculum? velitatur Fortuna eminus ac, nisi longe firmiter praecaves, mox comminus congredietur. perfidae lupulae magnis conatibus nefarias insidias tibi comparant, quarum summa est, ut te suadeant meos explorare vultus, quos, ut tibi saepe praedixi, non videbis si videris. ergo igitur si posthac pessimae illae lamiae noxiis animis armatae venerint—venient autem, scio—neque omnino sermonem conferas et, si id tolerare pro genuina simplicitate proque animi tui teneritudine non potueris, certe de marito nil quicquam vel audias vel respondeas: nam et familiam nostram iam propagabimus et hic adhuc infantilis uterus gestat nobis infantem alium, si texeris nostra secreta silentio, divinum, si profanaveris, mortalem.'

12. nuntio Psyche laeta florebat et divinae subolis solacio plaudebat et futuri pignoris gloria gestiebat et materni nominis dignitate gaudebat: crescentes dies et menses exeuntes anxia numerat, et sarcinae nesciae rudimento miratur de brevi punctulo tantum incrementulum locupletis uteri.

sed iam pestes illae taeterrimaeque Furiae anhelantes vipereum virus et festinantes impia celeritate navigabant. tunc sic iterum momentarius maritus suam Psychen admonet: 'dies ultima et casus extremus: et sexus infestus et sanguis inimicus iam sumpsit arma et castra commovit et aciem direxit et classicum personavit; iam mucrone destricta iugulum tuum nefariae tuae sorores petunt. heu quantis urguemur cladibus, Psyche dulcissima! tui nostrique miserere, religiosaque continentia domum, maritum, teque et istum parvulum nostrum imminentis ruinae infortunio libera, nec illas scelestas feminas, quas tibi post internecivum odium et calcata sanguinis foedera sorores appellare non licet, vel videas vel audias, cum in morem Sirenum scopulo prominentes funestis vocibus saxa personabunt.'

13. suscipit Psyche singultu lacrimoso sermonem incertans: 'iamdudum, quod sciam, fidei atque parciloquio meo perpendisti documenta, nec eo setius approbabitur tibi nunc etiam firmitas animi mei. tu modo Zephyro nostro rursum praecipe fungatur obsequio, et in vicem denegatae sacrosanctae imaginis tuae redde saltem conspectum sororum. per istos cinnameos et undique pendulos crines tuos, per teneras et teretes et mei similes genas, per pectus nescio quo calore fervidum, sic in hoc saltem parvulo cognoscam faciem tuam: supplicis anxiae piis precibus erogatus germani complexus indulge fructum et tibi devotae dicataeque Psychae animam gaudio recrea. nec quicquam amplius in tuo vultu requiro, iam nil officiunt mihi nec ipsae nocturnae tenebrae: teneo te meum lumen.' his verbis et amplexibus mollibus decantatus maritus, lacrimasque eius suis crinibus detergens, se facturum spopondit et praevertit statim lumen nascentis diei.

14. iugum sororium consponsae factionis, ne parentibus quidem visis, recta de navibus scopulum petunt illum praecipiti cum velocitate, nec venti ferentis oppertae praesentiam, licentiosa cum temeritate prosiliunt in altum. nec immemor Zephyrus regalis edicti, quamvis invitus, susceptas eas gremio spirantis aurae solo reddidit. at illae incunctatae statim conferto vestigio domum penetrant, complexaeque praedam suam sororis nomen ementientes thesaurumque penitus abditae fraudis vultu laeto tegentes sic adulant: 'Psyche, non ita ut pridem parvula, et ipsa iam mater es. quantum, putas, boni nobis in ista geris perula, quantis gaudiis totam domum nostram hilarabis! o nos beatas quas infantis aurei nutrimenta laetabunt! qui si parentum, ut oportet, pulchritudini responderit, prorsus Cupido nascetur.'

15. sic affectione simulata paulatim sororis invadunt animum; statimque eas a lassitudine viae sedilibus refotas et balnearum vaporosis fontibus curatas pulcherrime, triclinio mirisque illis et beatis edulibus atque tuccetis oblectat. iubet citharam loqui, psallitur; tibias agere, sonatur; choros canere, cantatur: quae cuncta nullo praesente dulcissimis modulis animos audientium remulcebant. nec tamen scelestarum feminarum nequitia vel ipsa mellita cantus dulcedine mollita conquievit, sed ad destinatam fraudium pedicam sermonem conferentes dissimulanter occipiunt sciscitari qualis ei maritus et unde natalium, secta cuia proveniret. tunc illa simplicitate nimia pristini sermonis oblita, novum commentum instruit aitque maritum suum de provincia proxima magnis pecuniis negotiantem iam medium cursum aetatis agere, interspersum rara canitie. nec in sermone isto tantillum morata rursum opiparis muneribus eas onustas ventoso vehiculo reddidit.

16. sed dum Zephyri tranquillo spiritu sublimatae domum redeunt, sic secum altercantes: 'quid, soror, dicimus de tam monstruoso fatuae illius mendacio? tunc adolescens modo florenti lanugine barbam instruens, nunc aetate media candenti canitie lucidus: quis ille quem temporis modici spatium repentina senecta reformavit? nil aliud repperies, mi soror quam vel mendacia istam pessimam feminam confingere vel formam mariti sui nescire; quorum utrum verum est, opibus istis quam primum exterminanda est. quodsi viri sui faciem ignorat, deo profecto denupsit et deum nobis praegnatione ista gerit. certe si divini puelli—quod absit—haec mater audierit, statim me laqueo nexili suspendam. ergo interim ad parentes nostros redeamus, et exordio sermonis huius quam concolores fallacias adtexamus.'

17. sic inflammatae, parentibus fastidienter appellatis et nocte turbatis, vigiliis perditae matutino scopulum pervolant et inde solito venti praesidio vehementer devolant, lacrimisque pressura palpebrarum coactis, hoc astu puellam appellant: 'tu quidem felix et ipsa tanti mali ignorantia beata, sedes incuriosa periculi tui; nos autem, quae pervigili cura rebus tuis excubamus, cladibus tuis misere cruciamur. pro vero namque comperimus nec te, sociae scilicet doloris casusque tui, celare possumus immanem colubrum multinodis voluminibus serpentem, veneno noxio colla sanguinantem hiantemque ingluvie profunda, tecum noctibus latenter acquiescere. nunc recordare sortis Pythicae, quae te trucis bestiae nuptiis destinatam esse clamavit: et multi coloni, quique circumsecus venantur, et accolae plurimi viderunt eum vespera redeuntem e pastu proximique fluminis vadis innatantem.

18. nec diu blandis alimoniarum obsequiis te saginaturum omnes affirmant, sed cum primum praegnationem tuam plenus maturaverit uterus, opimiore fructu praeditam devoraturum. ad haec iam tua est existimatio, utrum sororibus pro tua cara salute sollicitis assentiri velis et declinata morte nobiscum secura periculi vivere, an saevissimae bestiae sepeliri visceribus: quodsi te ruris huius vocalis solitudo vel clandestinae Veneris faetidi periculosique concubitus et venenati serpentis amplexus delectant, certe piae sorores nostrum fecerimus.'

tunc Psyche misella, utpote simplex et animi tenella, rapitur verborum tam tristium formidine: extra terminum mentis suae posita prorsus omnium mariti monitionum suarumque promissionum memoriam effudit et in profundum calamitatis sese praecipitavit, tremensque et

exsangui colore lurida tertiata verba semihianti voce substrepens sic
ad illas ait:

19. 'vos quidem, carissimae sorores, ut par erat, in officio vestrae
pietatis permanetis, verum et illi qui talia vobis affirmant non videntur
mihi mendacium fingere: nec enim umquam viri mei vidi faciem vel
omnino cuiatis sit novi, sed tantum nocturnis subaudiens vocibus
maritum incerti status et prorsus lucifugam tolero, bestiamque
aliquam recte dicentibus vobis merito consentio: meque magnopere
semper a suis terret aspectibus, malumque grande de vultus curiositate
praeminatur. nunc si quam salutarem opem periclitanti sorori vestrae
potestis afferre, iam nunc subsistite; ceterum incuria sequens prioris
providentiae beneficia corrumpit.'

tunc nanctae iam portis patentibus nudatum sororis animum
facinerosae mulieres, omissis tectae machinae latibulis, districtis gladiis
fraudium simplicis puellae paventes cogitationes invadunt.

20. sic denique altera: 'quoniam nos originis nexus pro tua incolumitate
ne periculum quidem ullum ante oculos habere compellit, viam quae
sola deducit iter ad salutem diu diuque cogitatam monstrabimus tibi.
novaculam praeacutam, appulsu etiam palmulae lenientis exasperatam,
tori qua parte cubare consuesti, latenter absconde lucernamque
concinnem, completam oleo, claro lumine praemicantem subde aliquo
claudentis aululae tegmine, omnique isto apparatu tenacissime
dissimulato, postquam sulcatos intrahens gressus cubile solitum
conscenderit iamque porrectus et exordio somni prementis implicitus
altum soporem flare coeperit, toro delapsa nudoque vestigio pensilem
gradum paullulatim minuens, caecae tenebrae custodia liberata
lucerna, praeclari tui facinoris opportunitatem de luminis consilio
mutuare et ancipiti telo illo audaciter, prius dextera sursum elata, nisu
quam valido noxii serpentis nodum cervicis et capitis abscinde. nec
nostrum tibi deerit subsidium; sed cum primum illius morte salutem

tibi feceris, anxiae praestolabimur, cunctisque istis opibus tecum relatis votivis nuptiis hominem te iungemus homini.'

21. tali verborum incendio flammata viscera sororis iam prorsus ardentis deserentes ipsae protinus, tanti mali confinium sibi etiam eximie metuentes, flatus alitis impulsu solito porrectae super scopulum, ilico pernici se fuga proripiunt statimque conscensis navibus abeunt.

at Psyche relicta sola, nisi quod infestis Furiis agitata sola non est, aestu pelagi simile maerendo fluctuat, et quamvis statuto consilio et obstinato animo, iam tamen facinori manus admovens adhuc incerta consilii titubat multisque calamitatis suae distrahitur affectibus. festinat, differt; audet, trepidat; diffidit, irascitur; et, quod est ultimum, in eodem corpore odit bestiam, diligit maritum. vespera tamen iam noctem trahente praecipiti festinatione nefarii sceleris instruit apparatum: nox aderat et maritus aderat primusque Veneris proeliis velitatus altum soporem descenderat.

22. tunc Psyche et corporis et animi alioquin infirma fati tamen saevitia subministrante viribus roboratur, et prolata lucerna et adrepta novacula sexum audacia mutatur.

sed cum primum luminis oblatione tori secreta claruerunt, videt omnium ferarum mitissimam dulcissimamque bestiam, ipsum illum Cupidinem formonsum deum formonse cubantem, cuius aspectu lucernae quoque lumen hilaratum increbruit et acuminis sacrilegi novaculam paenitebat. at vero Psyche tanto aspectu deterrita et impos animi marcido pallore defecta tremensque desedit in imos poplites et ferrum quaerit abscondere, sed in suo pectore; quod profecto fecisset, nisi ferrum timore tanti flagitii manibus temerariis delapsum evolasset. iamque lassa, salute defecta, dum saepius divini vultus intuetur pulchritudinem, recreatur animi. videt capitis aurei genialem caesariem ambrosia temulentam, cervices lacteas genasque purpureas pererrantes crinium globos decoriter impeditos, alios antependulos,

alios retropendulos, quorum splendore nimio fulgurante iam et ipsum
lumen lucernae vacillabat; per umeros volatilis dei pinnae roscidae
micanti flore candicant et quamvis alis quiescentibus extimae
plumulae tenellae ac delicatae tremule resultantes inquieta lasciviunt;
ceterum corpus glabellum atque luculentum et quale peperisse
Venerem non paeniteret. ante lectuli pedes iacebat arcus et pharetra et
sagittae, magni dei propitia tela.

23. quae dum insatiabili animo Psyche, satis et curiosa, rimatur atque
pertrectat et mariti sui miratur arma, depromit unam de pharetra
sagittam et punctu pollicis extremam aciem periclitabunda trementis
etiam nunc articuli nisu fortiore pupugit altius, ut per summam cutem
roraverint parvulae sanguinis rosei guttae. sic ignara Psyche sponte in
Amoris incidit amorem. tunc magis magisque cupidine fraglans
Cupidinis prona in eum efflictim inhians patulis ac petulantibus saviis
festinanter ingestis de somni mensura metuebat. sed dum bono tanto
percita saucia mente fluctuat, lucerna illa, sive perfidia pessima sive
invidia noxia sive quod tale corpus contingere et quasi basiare et ipsa
gestiebat, evomuit de summa luminis sui stillam ferventis olei super
umerum dei dexterum. hem audax et temeraria lucerna et amoris vile
ministerium, ipsum ignis totius deum aduris, cum te scilicet amator
aliquis, ut diutius cupitis etiam nocte potiretur, primus invenerit. sic
inustus exiluit deus visaque detectae fidei colluvie prorsus ex osculis
et manibus infelicissimae coniugis tacitus avolavit.

24. at Psyche statim resurgentis eius crure dextero manibus ambabus
adrepto sublimis evectionis adpendix miseranda et per nubilas plagas
penduli comitatus extrema consequia tandem fessa delabitur solo. nec
deus amator humi iacentem deserens involavit proximam cupressum
deque eius alto cacumine sic eam graviter commotus adfatur:

'ego quidem, simplicissima Psyche, parentis meae Veneris praeceptorum
immemor, quae te miseri extremique hominis devinctam cupidine

infimo matrimonio addici iusserat, ipse potius amator advolavi tibi. sed hoc feci leviter, scio, et praeclarus ille sagittarius ipse me telo meo percussi teque coniugem meam feci, ut bestia scilicet tibi viderer et ferro caput excideres meum quod istos amatores tuos oculos gerit. haec tibi identidem semper cavenda censebam, haec benivole remonebam. sed illae quidem consiliatrices egregiae tuae tam perniciosi magisterii dabunt actutum mihi poenas, te vero tantum fuga mea punivero.' et cum termino sermonis pinnis in altum se proripuit.

Commentary Notes

Note: This commentary is heavily indebted to both the Cupid and Psyche volume in the Groningen Commentaries on Apuleius series, by Zimmerman et al. (2004), and Kenney (1990a); their influence should be assumed throughout, but where I have thought it worthwhile to draw out their particular insights, I have abbreviated them in the body of commentary simply as GCA and Kenney respectively.

Chapter 11

pro bono: 'as if it were good'; this is possibly just a repetition of the idea in *placet*, but could also be seen as a comment by the narrator, the old woman of the framing story; similarly, *proinde ut merebantur* provides (more clearly) the same narratorial moralizing judgement later in the same section.

duabus malis malum consilium: sc. *sororibus* (with *duabus malis*), in the dative after *placet*, with *malum consilium* as the subject. This the first example of polyptoton in this chapter, here highlighted by the chiasmus, and the kind of word-play Apuleius delights in.

totisque illis muneribus: ablative absolute (with *absconditis*). *totis* here = *omnibus* (this is not an uncommon substitution in Apuleius). The phrase refers back to a gift of jewels Psyche gave to her sisters at V.8.

comam trahentes: 'pulling out their hair', or more literally, 'tearing their hair'; the unusual phrase seems to have been borrowed from tragedy, perhaps a subtle reminder that the sisters are putting on an act.

ut merebantur: a similar phrase is used (of a single sister) at V.27; in both cases, the statement is introduced as the judgement of the narrator (herself an old woman within the story).

fletus: accusative plural, with *simulatos*.

ac sic. . .insontem: the language of this passage is echoed at V.27, where the sisters rush to their grisly deaths: *vesania* is echoed in the latter passage by *vesanae libidinis et invidiae noxiae*, and similar verbs of 'rushing' are used. The subject of the sentence is the sisters, with *parentes* the object of *deserentes*.

redulcerato: a very rare verb, appearing only once elsewhere in Latin literature as a technical medical term for the effect of rubbing pumice on a scab. Apuleius had written at least one treatise on medicine, when he perhaps came across the term; he is fond of using technical terminlogy in his writing, and elsewhere (like here with *dolore*) describes emotional pain in vividly physical terms (see IV.25 for another example). Along with its modifier *prorsum* the whole phrase could be translated as 'with the pain having been completely scratched open again'.

turgidae: often used of things which arouse the emotions, although only used one other time in the tale, in the literal sense of Psyche's pregnancy (at VI.9); here, used with the ablative *vesania*, 'swollen with madness'.

parricidium: in a strict technical sense the killing of a close relative, though often used in literature in a broader sense. Here, it is used in a sense very close to its technical legal one to highlight the heinousness of the sisters' plans.

insontem: placed in an emphatic final position in the sentence, and used in the poetic sense of 'doing no injury, harmless'.

maritus ille, quem nescit: the emphasis of *ille* is on the relative clause: the plot of the story hinges around the fact that her husband remains unknown, and references to Psyche's lack of knowledge build up to V.22, when she tragically discovers who her lover is. The audience, on the other hand, have been given enough hints from the oracle in IV.33 onwards for them to guess the identity of Cupid.

videsne: literally 'do you see. . .?' but the implication of this rhetorical question is that presumably she is not aware of the danger; we need to read a negative nuance into the question, and thus Kenney suggests it is best translated by 'Do you not see. . .?' There is no verb in the indirect question; supply *sit*, 'there is'.

velitatur Fortuna eminus. . .comminus congredietur: similar military imagery is used at V.12.4, V.14.3, V.15.1 and V.19.5; there is some irony here, as it usually Cupid's pursuits which are depicted in military terms.

Here, it is the personified Fortune depicted as the attacking party: *fortuna* is often depicted as a hostile force in the *Metamorphoses*. There is a similar warning about *fortuna* at V.5 (without the personification). *Fortuna* is, however, personified by the complaining sisters at the start of V.9, in their jealousy of Psyche (*en orba et saeva et iniqua Fortuna!*), and used (ironically?) by them to describe Psyche's good luck in V.10.

The martial verbs are given particular prominence here by their position at each end of Cupid's speech, and the chiastic pattern with their adverbs, giving the sense of an ordered and disciplined military assault – even more so with the marked alliteration and assonance of the final two words.

longe: could be construed either with *firmiter* = 'especially firmly', or with the verb, 'take precautions from far off'; whilst the former is certainly the better for a translation (and has parallels with other passages of the *Metamorphoses* for its likely meaning), Apuleius is no doubt making word-play with adverbs of distance in *eminus . . . longe . . . comminus*.

perfidae...respondeas: these two sentences are full of rhetorical verve: notice the marked assonance of 'a' and the polyptoton of *videbis...videris* and *venerint...venient*.

lupulae: a diminutive form of *lupa*, literally 'wolf', but often used of prostitutes; here, the undertones of preying on the helpless are probably foregrounded. Diminutives become more and more common in the Latin of Apuleius' time, but in this case might convey something of contempt: colourful translations would be appropriate here, but 'hags' or 'witches' convey the force well.

magnis conatibus: best translated as singular, 'with great effort'. A formulaic phrase of elevated rhetoric, used often in great historical speeches in Livy; it continues the military language used of Fortune, but in a contrast to the register of *lupulae*, and to the bathetic goal of simply seeing his face. This kind of stylistic contrast and variation was a popular aesthetic trick of authors of Apuleius' period.

nefarias: 'unspeakable', both in the colloquial sense of 'wicked', but probably also (as in English) a subtle etymological pun on 'not speaking' (the adjective is derived from *nefas*, connected to the root of *for, fari*, 'speak'): Cupid is advising Psyche not to speak to her sisters, and not to speak about him.

quarum summa est: *quarum* refers back to *insidias*, 'the point of which...' or 'the gist of which...'

te suadeant: notice that *suadeo* here, in contravention of the rules of classical Latin, is taking a direct object and an infinitive.

explorare: 'to reconnoitre' or 'to scout out', another military term; also note further down *armatae*.

meos...vultus, quos: *vultus* is a fourth declension noun, here in the accusative plural, though should be translated as singular, 'face'.

non videbis si videris: 'you will not see [again], if you see it'. *videris* is future perfect; these future perfects (as with *venerint* and *potueris* below) in the protases of conditionals are best translated as present tenses in English, although in strictly logical terms the Latin makes more sense.

ergo igitur: a pleonasm, flagging the hyper-rhetorical style of the speech.

lamiae: witches or monsters, used to scare children, chosen here possibly for the alliteration and assonance of *illae lamiae*. It also gives the sense that Cupid is talking down to Psyche as if she is a child, picked up later by the description of her *simplicitate* and *temeritudine*, and the reference to her *infantilis uterus*.

venerint...potueris: both future perfect, as *videris* above. Translate (as with *videris*) as a present.

neque omnino...nil quicquam: both reinforced negatives, 'don't at all', 'nothing at all'; the style of this is both indicative of colloquial speech and forceful.

conferas...vel audias vel respondeas: all present subjunctives of prohibition, equivalent to *noli conferre*, etc. In classical Latin, the last two alternatives should be presented by *aut...aut*, which is used (as is the case here) to mark sharp or exclusive alternatives, whereas *vel* treats the distinction as unimportant, and does not exhaust the potential alternatives. Apuleius, however, commonly uses *vel* like this.

pro genuina simplicitate proque...teneritudine: *pro* here = 'on account of', 'owing to'. This is the first appearance of the term *simplicitate*, which becomes a key characteristic for Psyche, and a point of contrast to her sisters: the simple girl is laid low by their guileful *artes*. *teneritudo* 'tenderness' is a very rare word, originally a technical term for the easily workable nature of soil; here, the agricultural background of the term plays with the idea of Psyche's fertility and foreshadows the mention of her pregnancy in the next sentence.

si texeris...divinum, si profanaveris, mortalem: the conditional clauses each apply to the following adjective; these in turn are modifiers of the *infantem* of the main clause: 'if you cover... [her uterus is bearing a] divine [child]' etc. This is a rare circumstance of a protasis in the future perfect tense depending on present tense verbs, characteristic of familiar speech. It makes the conditional emphatic, and foregrounds the dependence of the future occurrence on specific action (here, whether or not she keeps his identity secret). It is easier to translate this simply as if the apodoses were '*divinus erit...mortalis erit*'.

Chapter 12

nuntio: ablative; can be translated as 'at the announcement...'

laeta: the adjective here is predicative: that is, taken with the verb, rather than simply describing the noun. Thus: 'Psyche bloomed happy', or (in smoother English), 'Psyche bloomed with happiness'. Along with other agricultural vocabulary here (such as *subolis*) and earlier, Psyche is made to seem like a plant about to bear fruit.

florebat: in Latin, this is almost exclusively used of plants, and applied to a person as here is very rare.

solacio plaudebat: either an ablative of cause: 'she clapped her hands at...' or with a different sense of the verb, a dative: 'she was contented with herself for...' The divine child is a 'consolation' for the silence which Psyche must keep with her sister.

pignoris: the literal meaning of this is a pledge or security, in a commercial or legal sense, but comes to be used to refer to children or other relatives, as pledges or guarantees of love. Ominously, in earlier elegy, it is used of women who are about to or have already died (e.g. Prop. IV.11.73, Ovid *Epis.* 11.113, 12.192).

crescentes dies et menses exeuntes: note the chiastic arrangement of the phrase; the 'growing' and 'departing' remind us of her growing womb, and look forward to her child exiting the womb.

exeuntes: pres. ppl. of the verb *exeo*.

nesciae: normally, *nescius* is active in meaning – i.e., 'unknowing, ignorant, unaware', but here, it is used in a rare, archaic, passive sense, 'unknown' or 'unfamiliar'.

rudimento: causal or instrumental ablative; it could be translated as 'through/with/ because of the new experience ...'

de brevi punctulo: along with *incrementulum, punctulum* is a neologism: both forms are diminutives. They help create a sense of Psyche's naiveté, introduced by her wonder (*miratur*). The 'brief little prick' refers both to the prick of Cupid's arrow, but also refers to the sexual act of impregnation or defloration.

tantum incrementulum: a striking oxymoron.

illae: used here (as often in forensic oratory) in an accusatory fashion.

pestes...Furiae...virus: the sisters are figured both as some kind of disease, and as mythological monsters – here, the furies, terrifying goddesses of vengeance; they were often depicted with snakes for their hair. Notice also the alliteration of *vipereum virus*.

iterum: this is the fourth warning that Cupid has given (the earlier ones at V.5, V.6, and V.11).

momentarius: usually 'brief', here in reference to his fleeting visits, and possibly looking forward with irony to his impending departure.

suam: a familiar, intimate, way of describing Psyche, in contrast to *momentarius*.

dies ultima et casus extremus: some editions of the text have amended the text to make this an exclamation: *en dies ultima et casus extremus!* 'Behold, the final day and the final fall!' The text printed here treats this whole sentence as a tetracolon, with an unusual zeugma, where *dies* and *casus* are the subject (along with *sexus* and *sanguis*), even though logically they do not seem to apply to the verbs (*sumpsit, commovit* etc.). Along with the alliteration, anaphora, epic vocabulary and homoioteleuton in this section, the effect is one of over-the-top grandeur. The use of obviously military terminology compounds this effect.

personavit: an unusual late Latin form; the usual classical perfect of *persono* is *personui*.

tui nostrique miserere: *nostri* is genitive of *nos*; along with *tui*, following *miserere*, which takes the genitive. The plural *nos* is used to refer to the singular, i.e. Cupid referring to himself. *miserere* is imperative, from the deponent verb *miseror*.

religiosaque continentia: ablative of means.

istum parvulum nostrum: literally 'that little thing of ours', referring to their child in utero.

infortunio: ablative of separation ('from').

libera: imperative of *libero* (not feminine of *liber*).

nec…videas vel audias: prohibitive subjunctives, continuing the series of entreaties from Cupid to Psyche; best translated as if imperatives: 'and do not …'

in morem: 'in the manner . . .'

Sirenum: genitive plural, 'of the Sirens': mythical creatures who lured sailors to shipwreck and death by the sweetness of their singing; see *Odyssey* 12; the simile continues for the rest of the sentence.

scopulo: ablative, 'over the cliff' (translate with *prominentes* 'leaning out over the cliff').

personabunt: used here transitively (with a direct object – *saxa*) denoting where the sound resonates.

Chapter 13

quod sciam: 'as far as I know' (*quod* here = *quoad*); here, it takes the subjunctive to give a restrictive meaning to the phrase.

fidei atque parciloquio meo. . .documenta: the datives are dependent on *docementa*; translate as 'the proofs *of . . .*'

perpendisti: pure perfect: 'you have weighed'; the metaphor is drawn from legal language.

eo: ablative of comparison: 'than this'.

nec eo setius approbabitur tibi nunc etiam firmitas animi mei: *tibi* is dative of agent ('by you'), following *approbabitur*, which has *firmitas* as its subject.

tu modo: emphatic introduction to the imperative; difficult to translate but can be rendered 'Just you . . .'

Zephyro nostro: dative dependent on *praecipe*.

fungatur: iussive subjunctive in parataxis with *praecipe*, conveying the content of the order. Note *fungor* takes the ablative *obsequio*.

per...per...per: 'by the...'; a prayer formula, beginning with invocations and moving on to requests. The prayer aspect is emphasized by the anaphora.

per teneras et teretes et mei similes: all describing *genas*.

mei: equivalent to *meis genis*; the dative is dependent on *similes*, 'like mine.'

nescio quo: *nescio quis/quid* is used in an assertion to denote uncertainty; literally, 'I know not who/what'; here best translated as 'some strange' or 'some unknown'.

sic...cognoscam: *sic* here follows the imperative and introduces the subjunctive as a wish: 'may I...' or 'let me...'

hoc saltem parvulo: referring to their unborn child; the ablative can be translated by 'in...'

germani complexus: genitive, dependent on *fructus*, 'enjoyment of...'

tibi: understood with both *devotae* and *dicatae*.

Psychae animam: 'the soul of Psyche'; ψυχή (*psychē*)is Greek for soul, or *anima*; Apuleius is making bilingual word-play.

gaudio: ablative, 'with joy'.

recrea: imperative.

nec quicquam: alternative form of *quidquam*, the neuter of *quisquam*; object of *requiro*. With *nec*, it can be translated as 'and...nothing'.

amplius: comparative neuter adjective, agreeing with *quicquam*: 'further'.

in: (here) 'as to...'

nil. . .nec = *nihil*: here used adverbially: 'not at all'. The *nec* further emphasizes the negative, rather than constituting a double negative, and is best left untranslated.

officiunt mihi nec ipsae nocturnae tenebrae: *tenebrae* is the subject; *officiunt* takes the dative *mihi*.

meum lumen: in apposition to *te*; both *teneo* and *lumen* have romantic and erotic connotations. Kenney also suggests there is an allusion to the language of mystical revelation here: in any case, there is certainly some irony using this term for her unknown, invisible lover.

his. . .mollibus: ablatives of means with the perfect passive participle *decantatus*. *mollibus* should be understood as describing both nouns in slightly different ways: an example of zeugma.

eius: fem. gen. sing. of *is*.

suis crinibus: ablative of instrument; *suus* always refers back to the subject of the sentence (i.e. here, *maritus*). Notice the juxtaposition of *eius* and *suis*, brought together by the chiasmus of *lacrimas eius suis crinibus*. Her plea, earlier in the chapter, praying to him by his hair and cheeks, is echoed in his response.

se facturum [sc. esse]: an accusative and (future) infinitive construction dependent on *spopondit*.

spopondit: perfect of *spendeo*; the word has solemn legal connotations, suggesting a formal oath.

Chapter 14

iugum sororium: like English, a technically singular collective noun can take a plural verb; hence *iugum* takes *petunt*. *iugum* suggests the sisters working in tandem, but is also literally a 'yoke' for oxen, suggesting bestial qualities. Cf. *Sirenum* at V.12, and below on *complexae*.

consponsae factionis: a genitive of definition; translate as 'forming a pledged conspiracy'.

ne parentibus quidem visis: *ne...quidem* taken together; *parentibus visis*: ablative absolute.

recta: adverb.

illum: with *scopulum*.

praecipiti cum velocitate: read as *cum praecipiti velocitate* (remembering that third declension adjectives end in –*i*, not –*e* in the ablative singular). This foreshadows their eventual fate at V.27.

ferentis: this bears the meaning both of 'carrying' but also 'favourable'.

oppertae: fem. nom. plural perf. pass. part. of *opperior*. Elsewhere, the word is used solely in military contexts of soldiers awaiting their leader.

praesentiam: often used of the presence of gods; here, it refers to the sisters waiting for Zephyrus, who will carry them to Psyche.

licentiosa cum temeritate = *cum licentiosa temeritate*: as earlier, a foreshadowing of their fate.

in altum: 'into the air'; *altum* is often used both for the 'depths' of the sea, but also for the 'depths' of the sky.

immemor: like most verbs and adjectives of remembering/forgetting, with a genitive. The theme of remembering and forgetting recurs throughout the tale: cf. V.15, *pristini sermoni oblita*, and V.24, *praeceptorum immemor*.

regalis edicti: probably referring to Cupid's order, following his promise in V.13.

gremio: abl. = 'in...'; take with *susceptas*.

solo: dative of *solum*, 'ground'.

conferto vestigio: 'in close order', another military phrase for the sisters, as is *domum penetrant*.

complexaeque praedam suam: perfect active participle, 'having embraced'; the sisters are figured as serpents, wrapping round their prey; *praeda* is both military, the spoils taken in war, and bestial, prey caught in the chase.

sororis nomen ementientes: lit. 'uttering falsely the name of sister', i.e. laying false claim to the title of sister.

thesaurumque: although referring here to the 'riches' of the sister's deception, it reminds the reader of the greed of the sisters for Psyche's riches; the theme continues with their speeches, replete with metaphorical uses of gold and jewels.

adulant: in classical Latin, this would be the deponent *adulantur*; it continues the bestial undertones of the sisters, as the meaning properly is to fawn like a dog.

ut: here, 'as'.

parvula: a word-play with *perula*, below. Notice also the strong alliteration of *p* and *t* at the start of this speech.

et: possibly adversative here (= *sed*), but more likely explicative, 'as indeed...'

ipsa: as the verb is second person, *ipsa* here = you yourself.

quantum...boni: *boni* is a partitive genitive, used substantively; translate simply as agreeing with *quantum* ('how great a good').

putas: is parenthetical, as if in brackets; this kind of parataxis is typical of informal, familiar speech.

in ista...perula: translate together.

o nos beatas: the accusative is usually used in exclamations; English will normally supply a verb in an exclamation like this: 'How fortunate we are!'

quas infantis aurei nutrimenta laetabunt: here, a causal relative clause; in classical prose, it should be followed by a subjunctive. Translate: 'for the rearing of this golden child will bring joy to us'.

aurei: appropriate as both a general term for excellence, but also because Venus and Cupid are often given *aureus* as an epithet.

qui si: connective relative; translate 'If he ...'

parentum: gen. pl.; translate with *pulchritudini*.

ut oportet: 'as is bound to happen'; this is the explanatory use of *ut* with an indicative.

responderit: future perfect; necessary in Latin, as the protasis (the 'if' clause) happens in the future and logically precedes the apodosis; in English, it can be translated simply by the present, best translated here as 'measures up to' (followed by the dative *pulchritudini*).

prorsus: take here with *Cupido*.

Chapter 15

simulata: ablative (with *affectione*).

statimque…oblectat: the subject here changes to Psyche, with *eas* (the sisters, the object of *oblectat*) described with two parallel participial phrases (respectively dependent on *refotas* and *curatas*). The sentence is easiest to construe in sensible English if the participles are translated as if indicative verbs: i.e. 'she refreshed them…she attended to them…she delighted them…'

lassitudine viae: ablative of separation, 'from the weariness of the journey'.

fontibus: ablative of means dependent on *curatas*. *fontibus* is here equivalent to *aquis*, a poetic usage.

pulcherrime: construe with *curatas*.

triclinio: 'in the dining room'; the third in a tricolon of places – seats at the entrance hall, water at the bath, and now food at the table.

mirisque…et…atque: polysyndeton, equivalent simply to 'both…and'.

beatis: when used of food, *beatus* often takes the meaning 'rich', but there is possibly also a hint of the divine setting and origin of the hospitality.

citharam loqui…tibias agere…choros canere: a tricolon of indirect statements dependent on *iubet* (remembering that *iubeo*, unlike other verbs of ordering, is not followed by an indirect command). The asyndetic parataxis suggests the swift fulfilment of the commands. *loqui* here is a poetic usage, used to describe the sound of a musical instrument; likewise, *agere* has the particular meaning 'play, perform'.

psallitur…sonatur…cantatur: impersonal passives, lit. 'it is strummed', etc.; best translated as 'there is strumming…there is music…there is singing'.

quae cuncta: connective relative; best translated as if it were *haec cuncta*.

nullo praesente: ablative absolute; *nullus* here is substantival: 'no one'.

audientium: present participle used substantively: i.e. 'of those listening'.

nequitia...mollita: nominatives, in agreement. Notice the paronomasia with *mellita*.

vel: here is simply an intensifying particle: 'even'.

ipsa mellita cantus dulcedine: ablative phrase of means, dependent on *mollita*; *cantus* is genitive singular (4th decl.).

conferentes: (here) 'directing'; *sermonem* is the object.

qualis...unde...cuia proveniret: a series of three indirect questions, following *sciscitari*.

ei: possessive dative; here, feminine.

illa: nominative, with *oblita*.

simplicitate nimia: ablative; here, the force is 'out of' or 'owing to'.

pristini sermonis oblita: *obliviscor* takes a genitive.

novum commentum: as opposed to her earlier claim in V.8, in which her husband was young hunter.

de provincia proxima: in classical Latin, this would be *e* rather than *de*, meaning 'from'.

rursum: take with *onustas*.

ventoso vehiculo: this is Apuleius' only use of the adjective *ventosus*, undoubtedly to bring out the alliteration.

Chapter 16

tranquillo spiritu: metaphorical vocabulary is here used literally: normally, this would mean 'with a tranquil attitude', but here it means 'with [his] calm breath'. There is an element of irony: earlier (at V.14) we are told that Zephyrus is unhappy about carrying the sisters.

sublimatae: sc. *sorores*. The word is archaic, and emphasizes the divine nature of the sisters' travel.

domum: like the names of cities, towns, and small islands, *domus* without a preposition in the accusative can indicate direction towards.

secum: *se* always refers back to the subject; here 'among themselves'.

altercantes: the main verb of the sentence is missing (not uncommon for verbs of speaking in Apuleius); there are two options for translation; either simply translate *altercantes* as if it is the main verb, or add in a verb of speaking alongside the participle.

quid...dicimus: 'What are we to say?'; the question is really deliberative, which in classical Latin ought to be in the subjunctive; the use of the indicative is colloquial.

monstruoso fatuae illius mendacio: chiasmus: an ablative adjective-noun combination with a genitive adjective-noun in the midst of it. *fatuae illius* refers to Psyche.

tunc...nunc: can be translated literally, but has the sense 'one moment...the next'. Both halves of this neatly balanced sentence are full of nominal phrases, but are lacking verbs: supply *erat* to make sense in translation. See also below on *quis ille*.

florenti lanugine: both ablative.

instruens: an odd use of the verb; probably best understood here as 'growing'.

aetate media: a descriptive or qualifying ablative, 'of middle age'.

quis ille: supply *est*; the suppression of the verb *esse* (again) suggests a swift, urgent conversation.

temporis modici spatium: an example of hypallage; translate as if it reads *temporis modicum spatium*.

repentina senecta: ablative; an oxymoronic phrase; old age generally approaches slowly!

mi: equivalent to *mea*; in classical Latin, *mi* is the masculine vocative, but in later Latin like Apuleius is often used for the feminine also.

quam: following *aliud*, 'other than'.

feminam confingere: accusative infinitive construction dependent on *repperies*.

vel. . .vel: see note on Chapter 11 on *conferas. . . vel audias*.

quorum utrum: 'whichever of which' (*utrum* = *utrumque*); i.e. 'whichever of the two'.

opibus istis. . .exterminanda est: the gerundive of obligation, with Psyche as the subject, has dependent on it an ablative of separation: 'she must be banished from those riches of hers'.

denupsit: an unusual compound form of *nubo*, with attention drawn to it by alliteration of *denupsit. . .deum*. The force of the prefix is perhaps to emphasize her separation from her former home due to her marriage.

praegnatione: another rare word; the sisters use archaic, unusual expression to give force to the unusual nature of the marriage and pregnancy.

quod absit: a subjunctive of desire; *quod* refers to the situation in general, literally, 'may it be absent'. More colloquially, it could be translated 'God forbid!'

audierit: future perfect. *audio* is used here in the sense 'to be named'. This is most smoothly translated by taking *haec* ('she') as the subject and *mater* as a complement; i.e. 'if she is to be named the mother . . .'

redeamus: hortatory subjunctive, 'let us . . .'

exordio: dative, with *adtexamus*, 'let us weave into the beginning' (and possibly also with *concolores*, i.e. 'agreeing with the beginning').

quam concolores: in classical Latin, *quam* + superlative is a common intensifier ('as *x* as possible'); the usage is similar here, but with the positive form of the verb, 'of as similar a colour as possible'.

Chapter 17

sic inflammatae: referring to the preceding conversation; fire imagery is often used in description of the sisters; see, for example, V.21, *verborum incendio*.

parentibus. . .appellatis. . .turbatis: an ablative absolute, both participles agreeing with *parentibus*.

nocte: ablative of time at which.

vigiliis perditae: the text here is difficult to interpret, and may well be corrupt. As it stands as punctuated in this text, *perditae* is used in the sense 'ruined' with a causal ablative *vigiliis*.

matutino: translate as an adverb (an adverbial ablative).

scopulum: an accusative of direction (as if it were *ad scopulum*).

pervolant. . .devolant: the repetition (with variation) underscores the haste of the sisters.

lacrimisque. . .coactis: ablative absolute. This is the third visit of the sisters; in their second visit (V.14) they feigned joy, now they feign sorrow.

tu quidem. . .nos autem: the sisters set up a sharp contrast between themselves and Psyche.

felix et. . .beata: the sisters are using a formula familiar to ancient audience from *makarismos*-phrases, a conventional speech of praise, often within a religious or divine context. The effect here is sarcastic.

ipsa. . .ignorantia: ablative of cause, dependent on *beata*; can be translated here 'because of . . .'

incuriosa periculi tui: *incuriosus* takes a genitive, 'without concern for'. Both *ignorantia* and *incuriosa* betray authorial irony: it is eventually Psyche's lack of understanding of her husband's goodness, and her over-curiosity that leads to her downfall.

rebus tuis excubamus: there is some ambiguity here; the sisters intend for it to mean 'we keep watch over your affairs', but it can also be interpreted to mean 'we have our eyes on your possessions', which the reader knows, given the sisters' greed and envy, is the truth.

pro vero: 'as a fact'. The phrase most often occurs when something false is being presented as the truth.

comperimus: could be either present or perfect tense, but is clearly perfect here.

te. . .celare: *celo* takes an accusative of the person from which something is hidden.

sociae: nominative, in apposition to the first-person subject: 'we, the companions ...'

scilicet: 'of course', 'as you know', gives the feel of real speech, but is also potentially ironic: as readers, we know much better than Psyche the reasons for the sisters' approach.

immanem colubrum...acquiescere: indirect statement dependent on both *comperimus* and *celare*. The description of the snake is built up from various descriptions of mythic snakes in Latin poetry, most notably Virgil's snakes from the Laocoön episode in *Aeneid* II: the sisters are going all-out to terrify Psyche, but Apuleius is also demonstrating his literary credentials.

serpentem: although *serpens* can be used as a substantive, 'serpent', here it is the participle, 'creeping' (although Apuleius is clearly playing with the ambiguity); its manner of creeping is described with the preceding ablative phrase, *multinodis voluminibus.*

colla: (poetic) plural used for singular; this is an accusative of respect, dependent on *sanguinantem*; literally, 'blood-red in respect of its neck', but it can be rendered more smoothly in English, 'its neck blood-red ...'

latenter acquiescere: after the gruesome description of the snake, the end of the sentence is an almost comic anti-climax (bathos). *latenter* here has the force 'without your realizing it'.

recordare: the imperative of *recordor.*

sortis Pythicae: the prophecy referred to was given at IV.32: see the Introduction, p. 14. The oracle was not the Pythian oracle at Delphi, however, but the Milesian oracle. Is this just a slip by Apuleius, or is the reference to 'Pythian' Apollo, i.e. Apollo the Python-slayer, apt here?

quique: qui + que = 'and those who' (rather than from *quisque, quaeque, quodque*).

et multi coloni, quique...et accolae plurimi: the number of (fictional) witnesses is emphasized by the polysyndeton in this tricolon, as well as the build-up of *multi...plurimi*.

viderunt: the sisters appeal to Psyche's curiosity (see above on *incuriosa periculi tui*): her great desire is to see her husband.

Chapter 18

te saginaturum omnes affirmant: *omnes* refers to the 'witnesses' from the previous sentence. The rest of the sentence is an indirect statement dependent on *affirmant*, with Psyche's husband the implied subject (the accusative of the accusative + infinitive statement) and the *esse* of the future infinitive missing – read as *omnes affirmant [illum] te saginaturum [esse]...*

devoraturum: sc. *esse*, continuing the indirect statement.

ad haec: 'in respect of these things', 'in light of these facts'.

tua est existimatio: lit. 'the judgement is yours', i.e. 'it's up to you to judge...', followed by an alternative indirect question (*utrum...velis...an...*).

pro tua cara salute: another instance of authorial irony with *cara*; the reader knows that the sisters are not concerned with her 'precious safety' but with her 'precious' riches.

declinata morte: ablative absolute.

secura periculi: *secura* is nominative and here takes a genitive of the source of the fear; the adjective is used predicatively, 'to live safe from danger'.

saevissimae bestiae sepeliri visceribus: note the heavy sibilance of the line; *velis* must be understood again, governing the infinitive *sepeliri*. The latter half of this line is a quotation of the first-century BC philosophical poet Lucretius (*De rerum natura* 5.993), which talks about uncivilized early humans eating their food alive.

vocalis: can be construed either as a nominative, with *solitudo*, or as a genitive, with *ruris huius*. The meaning is not altered drastically either way – 'the musical solitude of this countryside' (Kenney) or 'this voice-filled country seat's desolation' (GCA, slightly adapted). The sisters are referring to the invisible voices which surround and serve Psyche.

amplexus: nominative plural (as shown by the plural verb). The sisters are playing on the possible meanings of the word – either romantic embraces, or the coilings of a snake around its victim.

nostrum: here, 'our duty'.

misella: this is a frequently occurring epithet for Psyche, right from the beginning of her story at IV.34. Like *tenella* later in the sentence, it is a diminutive, and helps create pity for Psyche; note the homoioteleuton between the two.

animi tenella: 'tender of mind'; the same phrase is used below at V.22, and forms a contrast to what she has assured Cupid of at V.13 – *firmitas animi*.

formidine: as well as the 'terror' the sisters' speech evokes, *formido* is also the word for a rope with feathers attached used for hunting (see Virgil *Aeneid* XII.750) – Psyche is her sisters' prey.

extra terminum mentis suae posita: Psyche remains the subject; *posita* is nominative.

in profundum calamitatis: the 'chasm' into which Psyche throws herself is metaphorical here, but it foreshadows the eventual deaths of the sisters, who throw themselves into a more literal abyss (V.27), as well as Psyche's own later attempts to commit suicide by throwing herself off a high place (V.25, VI.12, VI.17).

exsangui colore lurida: *lurida* is nominative, agreeing with Psyche, and explained by the preceding ablative phrase; paleness is one of the main signs of terror in classical literature.

tertiata verba: accusative, object of *substrepens*. *tertiare* was originally an agricultural term referring to ploughing the land for a third time, but was used since early Latin for repeating something three time; it conveys Psyche's uncertainty and fearfulness.

substrepens: an Apuleian coinage; *strepo* means to make a loud, inarticulate, noise, and tends to keep this meaning in compounds, but here it must mean 'muttering' or 'whispering'; one of Apuleius' characteristic neologisms, combining the idea of Psyche's inarticulacy with an onomatopoeia strengthened by the repetition of *s* in *semihianti* and *sic*.

Chapter 19

quidem...verum: acts here like a balanced pair; *verum* here is connective rather than adversative ('truly' with a force of 'and' rather than 'but').

ut par erat: 'as is proper'; this use of the imperfect indicative is slightly odd; commentators disagree about what it is technically (either a remote idea, or with the sense that this has been the case in the past and continues to be so), but this affects the translation or meaning little either way.

in officium...**permanetis**: *in officium permanere* is an official term meaning 'to remain on duty' or 'keep to one's job'; Apuleius extends its meaning here by adding the explanatory genitive phrase *vestrae pietatis.*

nec...**vel omnino**: 'neither...nor at all'.

viri mei: unlike in classical Latin, Apuleius' usual word for husband is *maritus*, not *vir*; its use here might be due to the alliteration of the syllable *vi*, but also possibly raises the question of whether he really is a husband at all (echoed by *maritum incerti status*).

cuiatis sit: subj. in indirect question, following *novi* (perfect in form but present in meaning). *cuiatis* is an archaic nominative (which would be *cuias* in classical Latin).

subaudiens: this compound normally means 'supply', but here must mean something like 'submitting to'; possibly Apuleius is copying a Greek word with that force, ὑπακούω (by a literal translation) which also takes a dative (like here – *nocturnis vocibus*).

tantum: adverbial, 'just', 'merely'.

status: genitive singular (fourth declension), agreeing with *incerti*; a genitive of specification. There is ambiguity to the phrase – does it mean 'of unknown physical form', 'of uncertain station in life', or 'of questionable status as a husband'? There is probably also some etymological word-play – *status* is connecting to *sto, stare*, and notions of staying and permanence, which contrasts *lucifugam*.

bestiamque aliquam: sc. *esse*; an accusative infinitive statement following *dicentibus*. Note the bestial connotations of *lucifugam*, with hints of a nocturnal animal, which precedes this explicit identification.

dicentibus vobis: dative following *consentio*, 'assent to you saying ...'

a suis terret aspectibus: not 'scares [me] with his appearances' but 'frightens [me] off from seeing him'; *suis* is a possessive adjective replacing an objective genitive (i.e. 'the appearances of him').

malumque grande: the object of *praeminatur,* 'he threatens me in advance with a mighty evil'.

de vultus curiositate: *de* is causal (a colloquial usage), 'as a result of'. *vultus* is a genitive (4th declension) of specification; 'about/with regard to his face'.

praeminatur: another Apuleian neologism formed by a novel addition of a prefix (cf. *substrepens* in Chapter 18).

quam salutarem opem: in a conditional clause, *quis* can stand for *quisquam,* 'any', 'anyone/anything'.

ceterum: adverbial, in a causal sense, 'for'.

incuria sequens prioris providentiae beneficia: *incuria* is the subject, modified by *sequens,* best translated here as 'subsequent'; *beneficia* is accusative plural, and has the genitive *prioris providentiae* dependent on it.

tunc nanctae. . .invadunt: see the Introduction, p. 29 on the markedly military language, and particularly its reminiscences of the fall of Troy as narrated by Aeneas in *Aeneid* II.

nanctae: perf. (active) part. of *nanciscor.*

portis patentibus: ablative absolute, as is *omissis tectae machinae latibulis* and *destrictis gladiis*; the last phrase is given the remarkable genitive of definition *fradium,* 'the swords of their deceptions'.

tectae machinae latibulis: *tectae* is the perfect passive participle of *tego,* with *machinae* 'of the covered machine'; the term *machina* is used by Virgil several times of the Trojan horse. The image is more broadly of besiegers who approach city walls under the cover of a *testudo*, a movable shelter made of wood to protect from missiles.

Chapter 20

altera: one (of the two); a verb of speaking needs to be assumed; this is rare in Apuleius, and gives a more dramatic opening to the speech.

nexus: nominative singular; *nos* is the object.

pro: here 'as regards . . .'

ne. . .quidem: for *nequidem*. The emphatic negative with *ullum*, literally, 'not even any' is used to convey the idea of 'not even the slightest' or 'not even any possible . . .'

ante oculos habere: literally 'to have before our eyes', but a common idiom to mean 'to keep in mind, be aware of'.

iter: is the object of *deducit*, 'leads your path' (GCA notes that it 'is difficult idiomatically').

diu diuque: an adverbial expression which occurs only in Apuleius; 'for a long, long time', which modifies the participle *cogitatam*; this participle (agreeing with *viam*) is best translated as if it is another relative clause, 'and which we have been considering'.

novaculam: Psyche almost kills herself using this same knife later on, at V.22.

appulsu etiam palmulae lenientis exasperatam: the whole phrase is dependent on *exasperatam*, and is a complex way of referring to a blade so sharp that it will cut when just passed gently over the hand to test it (so GCA); Kenney, however, interprets *exasperatam* not as the blade 'incited' to cut, but as being sharpened, 'the paradox that the gentle caressing motion of the hand imparts an additional edge'.

lenientis: used absolutely as an attribute (usually a feature of poetry) – 'your stroking palm'. There are two further similar uses of the present participle in this chapter; *claudentis aululae* ('an enclosed little pot') and *somni prementis* ('oppressive sleep').

tori qua parte = *qua parte tori*: the ablative is of place where; i.e. 'in that part of the bed where...' Postponing the relative pronoun is again indicative of poetic usage; the sister's speech is in high style.

consuesti: a syncopated perfect, for *consuesisti*.

subde: imperative of *subdo*, with its attendant ablative (*tegmine*) with the meaning 'under'.

aliquo claudentis aululae tegmine: this refers to what was probably a common practice of placing a lit lamp under a cover, to give temporary darkness without having to relight the lamp afterwards. Cf. *Matthew* 5:15, where the same image is used by Jesus. See above on *lenientis* for the use of the present participle.

omnique...dissimulato: ablative absolute.

sulcatos...gressus: accusative plural, object of *intrahens*. *sulcare* was used in earlier poetry as indicative of the trail a snake leaves: e.g. Ovid *Met.* 15.725, and Lucan IX.721.

cubile solitum: accusative, object of *conscenderit*.

conscenderit...coeperit: the verbs are future perfect; English prefers either a perfect or a present 'after he has ascended/he ascends'.

exordio...implicitus: 'enveloped in the beginning'.

somni prementis: see above on *lenientis* for the use of the present participle. *premo* is commonly used of sleep, but Kenney notes that with *simplicitus* it gives an image of wrestling.

toro: ablative of separation with *delapsa*, 'having slipped from the bed'.

nudoque vestigio: literally, 'with a naked footprint', but clearly *vestigium* here = *pedes*; this metonymy is rare and poetic (e.g. Virgil, *Aeneid* VII.689–90, Catullus 64.162).

pensilem: literally 'hanging'; the image is of the feet or toes being vertical, i.e. 'on tip-toe'.

gradum paullulatim minuens: 'shortening your stride little by little'. *paullulatim* is not attested elsewhere.

caecae tenebrae custodia: *custodia* is ablative of separation after *liberata* ('freed *from*...'), with the genitive *caecae tenebrae* dependent upon it.

The primary meaning of *caecus* is 'blind', and therefore by extension something that cannot be seen ('invisible'), or the conditions which obstruct sight – 'gloomy, obscure'. Its use here is clearly in this last, neutral sense, but it is almost possible to read this as a personification of the darkness, mirroring the personified lamp, suggested in the following *liberata lucerna*, and developed in V.22.

liberata lucerna: ablative absolute.

de luminis consilio: the genitive *luminis* intervenes between preposition and its noun; the phrase is dependent on *mutuare*, 'obtain from the counsel of the light'. *consilium* continues the personification of the lamp; its 'advice' here refers to the fact that it will allow Psyche to see what she's doing.

mutuare: passive imperative form (but active in meaning – *mutuor* is deponent).

ancipiti telo illo: ablative of means, 'with that two-edged weapon'.

dextera sursum elata: ablative absolute.

quam valido: intensifying; 'as strong as possible'; *valido* is ablative, agreeing with *nisu*.

nodum: literally a knot, but here the connective tendon between parts of the body. The precise description of body parts is reminiscent of Homeric battle scenes.

nostrum. . .subsidium: the subject of *deerit* (future of *desum*).

cum primum illius morte tibi salutem feceris: future perfect, but in English translated as a perfect: 'as soon as you have made safety for yourself'. This loose use of *facio* is colloquial. Note also the contrast brought out by the chiasmus of *illius mortem tibi salutem*.

cunctisque. . .relatis: ablative absolute.

votivis nuptiis: ablative of specification: 'in a longed-for marriage'. In classical Latin, *votivus* has the meaning 'offered in fulfilment of a vow', but in Later authors like Apuleius is used in the sense suggested here.

hominem te: in apposition: 'you, a human'. The polyptoton with *homini* emphasizes the sisters' argument that her husband is a monster, not a man; to the audience (and possibly to the sister herself? At V.9, the sisters had guessed the truth) the irony is that her lover is not a human being, but a god.

Chapter 21

tali. . .incendio flammata: 'enflamed by such a fire'; *flammata* is accusative neuter plural with *viscera* (although best translated by the singular 'heart'), the object of *deserentes*. While the meaning is clear, the phrasing does seem odd – 'leaving the heart of their sister. . .' There are strong similarities in this passage to Virgil's description of the sack of Troy, e.g. *Aen.* II.327; see above on Chapter 19, and the Introduction, p. 29; here, Psyche's heart is figured as the sacked and burning citadel.

sororis: *their* sister, i.e. Psyche; *ardentis* is a transferred epithet (or hypallage) – although it grammatically agrees with *soror*, in sense it agrees with *viscera*.

flatus alitis: genitive.

pernici. . .fuga: ablative, 'in swift flight'.

se. . .proripiunt: literally, 'they snatched themselves away'.

conscensis navibus: ablative absolute.

nisi quod: 'except for the fact that'.

infestis Furiis: referring to the sisters; cf. V.12.

aestu pelagi simile: *simile* is neuter accusative singular used adverbially, and is followed by the (irregular) dative *aestu:* 'as if on the tide of the sea'.

maerendo: ablative gerund: 'in her grief' (almost as if being used as a present participle).

quamvis statuto consilio et obstinato animo: both ablatives absolute. *quamvis* with a participle is not common in classical Latin, but is favoured by Apuleius. The whole phrase can be translated concessively, 'although her decision is made'.

facinori: dative, the indirect object of *manus* (accusative plural) *admovens*: 'applying her hands to the deed.'

incerta consilii: 'uncertain of her plan.'

multisque calamitatis suae distrahitur affectibus: the final part of a tricolon describing her emotional disturbance; each phrase builds in length (i.e. increasing numbers of syllables), and here the hyperbaton of *multis. . .affectibus* echoes her mental distress.

festinat, differt; audet, trepidat; diffidit, irascitur: Psyche's internal conflict is expressed with great rhetorical force; here, by three balanced asyndetic pairs, with clear alliteration of *f*. The sound of this section has been carefully constructed by Apuleius (see also the previous note). In this section, the verb forms gradually increas in length; altogether, there are seventeen syllables here; it is balanced, after a short bridging phrase, almost exactly by eighteen syllables in *in eodem corpore. . .maritum* (itself containing a strong asyndetic contrast with *odit bestiam, diligit maritum*).

vespera. . .trahente: ablative absolute.

nox aderat: this is reminiscent of epic, in which *nox erat* opens passages of anxious worry, or of dramatic events.

primusque: strictly speaking, an adjective describing *maritus*, but functionally here an adverb; it is best understood in relation with *tunc* later: 'first. . ., then . . .'

Veneris proeliis: there is a long literary tradition of equating love and sex with warfare; here, the metaphorical imagery carries irony, for the figurative battles of love are designed by Psyche to presage real physical violence.

Chapter 22

et corporis et animi: genitive of specification, with *infirma*: 'weak in body and soul'.

fati...saevitia subministrante: ablative absolute; sc. *vires*, 'with the cruelty of her fate supplying strength'. The difference between Fortune (*fortuna*) and Fate (*fatum*), and the various words associated with them (like *providentia*) are not demarcated as clearly distinguished forces in the *Metamorphoses*, at least until the clear *providentia* of Isis is revealed in Book XI.

viribus: ablative of specification, depending on *roboratur*, 'she is strengthened in might'; a sensible English translation might be 'she gains in strength'.

prolata lucerna et adrepta novacula: both ablatives absolute.

sexum audacia mutatur: the passive *mutatur* can be taken here as equivalent to a Greek middle, with an accusative *sexum*, 'she changes her sex in her daring'; alternatively, *sexum* might be an accusative of respect: 'she is changed by her daring in respect of her sex'. The alternatives give rise to different interpretations: is Psyche in control here, or just the passive victim of fate?

sed cum primum...secreta claruerunt: *secreta* is the subject, 'as soon as the secrets have been illuminated'. The vocabulary is somewhat reminiscent of the mystery religions, with initiations which often involved the viewing of secret, sacred objects. There is a thematic parallel with the conclusion of the *Metamorphoses* as a whole, in which Lucius is initiated into the *secreta* of Isis (cf. XI.11, XI.21). On this passage in general, see the analysis in the Introduction, p. 25.

omnium ferarum mitissimam dulcissimamque bestiam: this recalls and fulfills the words of the oracle at IV.33, that Psyche would marry something *saevum atque ferum vipereumque malum*. On the imagery of Cupid as savage and terrifying, see the Introduction, p. 18.

ipsum illum Cupidinem: the first time Cupid is named in the story; the combination *ipsum illum* adds extra emphasis to the naming, emphasizing Psyche's surprise; a well-read ancient audience, however, will have guessed from the oracle at IV.33 onwards who her lover was.

cuius aspectu: ablative of specification with the genitive relative pronoun; 'at the sight of whom ...'

lucernae...lumen: the personification of the lamp is made even clearer here; see further the notes on V.23. Its joy is contrasted to the shame of the knife (*novaculam paenitebat*).

acuminis sacrilegi: genitive of quality, the knife 'of sacrilegious sharpness'.

tanto aspectu deterrita: 'terrified by so great a sight'. Extra emphasis is added by the prefix *de-*, along with a number in the passage which give the strong impression of her shrinking back: *defecta, desedit, abscondere, delapsum, evolasset, defecta*.

marcido pallore defecta: either read together as a whole phrase, with an ablative of cause from *defecta*, 'overcome with the pallor of faintness' (thus Kenney); alternatively, the ablative phrase could be read independently to express a physical quality of Psyche: in the looser translation of the GCA: 'weakened and pale, she almost faints'. Her paleness is both indicative of fear, but is also classically the sign of a woman falling in love.

abscondere, sed in suo pectore: an instance of zeugma, with *abscondere* first taking the meaning of simply 'hide', and then its more violent colouring, 'thrust [a weapon into someone]'. This is the first of five suicide attempts by Psyche.

fecisset: a pluperfect subjunctive as the apodosis of a past counterfactual conditional; 'she would have done'.

nisi: here, translate as 'if. . .not' rather than 'unless'.

ferrum. . .evolasset: *evolasset* is syncopated pluperfect subjunctive: i.e. = *evolavisset*. The personification of the knife here gives an example of the pathetic fallacy, when inanimate objects or nature act in accordance with the emotions of the human characters in a narrative. There are different ways of explaining its effect here: it could represent the involuntary loss of muscular control as she is fainting; it might demonstrate that even the inanimate world recognizes the power of the divinity (as do the river and other helpers in her ordeals later in Book VI); or it could be gesturing towards a literary tradition of objects refusing to co-operate in murder (e.g. Ovid, *Fasti* III.51–2; *Metamorphoses* VIII.513).

timore tanti flagitii: 'out of fear of such a great crime'; either Psyche's suicide or the murder of her husband is meant.

salute defecta: 'bereft of salvation'; *deficio* takes an ablative of separation for being deprived or bereft of something.

divini vultus: genitive.

recreatur animi: *recreo* here is taking a genitive: 'she is restored in soul'. Note the echo of V.13, *Psychae animam gaudio recrea*, where Psyche hoped to restore her soul by being reunited with her sisters; the fulfilment of her wish is found in gazing at her husband. There are again hints of mystery religion here which link this section to the Isiac initiation in Book XI; at XI.22 Lucius is described as *recreatus animi* because of the commands of the goddess Isis, and the positive effect of gazing on the goddess is frequently mentioned in Book XI (e.g. XI.24). The references to the mysteries continue through the ecphrasis.

videt: placed prominently to mark the start of the ecphrasis of Cupid; see the Introduction, pp. 24–27.

capitis aurei: foreshadowed by *aurei* in V.14. Note the prevalence of words for colour and light.

genialem caesariem: much of this description, in fact, has been foreshadowed; Psyche swore by Cupid's locks and cheeks at V.13, and it was with his hair that Cupid later in V.13 dried her tears. *genialis* may mean 'rich' or 'joyful' but could also convey a sense of 'divine'.

ambrosia temulentam: 'drunk with ambrosia'; a combination of the divine aspects of Cupid, and one of the traditional attributes of a lover in elegiac poetry (drunk, both literally and figuratively).

cervices lacteas: the plural is the original form for the neck, the singular originally only being used poetically.

pererrantes: with *globos impeditos*: '[she sees] the tufts of hair, gracefully bound, wandering'. The carefully arranged disorder is echoed by the rhythm of the Latin: *pererrantes* is four syllables, balancing clauses of thirteen syllables on each side (*cervices... impeditos*).

alios antependulos, alios retropendulos: again, a careful use of isocolon (phrases of equal length), with two Apuleian coinages, shows a careful and deliberate artistic arrangement.

splendore nimio fulgurante: an ablative absolute used in a causal sense: 'because of the sheer amount of shining brilliance'. *nimius* here is not 'too much' but just a synonym for *multo*.

per umeros: 'on the shoulders'.

volatilis dei: 'of the winged god'; this again reminds the audience of the oracle at IV.33, where her lover is decribed as *pinnis volitans,* but also has the ambiguity of *volatilis* meaning 'fleeting, transient'; he is liable to flee, as he does in V.23.

micanti flore: an ablative of description, dependent on *candicant,* which is best captured in English with a simile: 'glow like a gleaming blossom'; along with *roscidae,* there is an implied comparison of the wings with a flower glistening with dew. Note also the alliteration of *c* and the assonance of *a* in this phrase. *flos* has a transferred meaning of 'brightness, lustre', which, along with the literal image, is probably also at play here.

quamvis alis quiescentibus: a concessive use of an ablative absolute, with *quamvis,* as above at V.21 with *quamvis statuto consilio.*

plumulae tenellae: the diminutives are visually descriptive of the 'delicate little feathers', but also add to the alliteration of *l.*

inquieta: neuter plural used adverbially, 'restlessly'.

ceterum corpus glabellum atque luculentum: sc. *erant.* Being *glabellus,* hairless, was a sign of ideal adolescent beauty in the ancient literature. Having dwelt excessively on the head and shoulders, finishing the ecphrasis in this swift and almost abrupt way is a typical motif.

quale peperisse Venerem non paeniteret: 'such as would not displease Venus to have brought forth'. *paeniteret* is a subjunctive in a relative clause of characteristic; the sequence of tenses would normally require a present subjunctive, coming after a present tense verb (*videt*) in the main clause, but as it is a historic present tense, the imperfect subjunctive can be used.

ante lectuli pedes: 'feet' used metaphorically, where in English we would say 'in front of the foot of the bed'.

iacebat: as is common when a list of subjects is given, the verb is singular if the nearest subject noun (*arcus*) is singular.

arcus et pharetra et sagittae, magni dei propitia tela: another isocolon to finish the ecphrasis, with ten syllables on each side of the comma. *propitia tela* is in apposition to the preceding tricolon – i.e. is nominative like *arcus, pharetra, sagittae*, and explains them in different terms.

Chapter 23

quae dum: connecting relative, accusative neuter plural with *tela* its antecendent; translate as if it were *dum Psyche haec rimatur*.

insatiabili animo: ablative of manner. The adjective always has negative connotations elsewhere in the *Metamorphoses*; the use of *animo* here builds on the development we saw in Chapter 22 with *impos animi* and *recreatur animi*. Note also we have the etymological Greek word-play again with *animus*/Psychē. Apuleius is foregrounding the philosophical, Platonic undercurrents of the story; in Plato's *Phaedrus* 252a, we are told the soul regrows its wings by contemplating physical beauty. See the Introduction, pp. 9–13 and 20–21.

satis et curiosa: here, simply used to mean 'very'; its use here may be prompted by the word-play of *insatiabili. . .satis*. The *et* is not joining *satis* and *curiosa* but rather intensifying: 'very curious as well'.

rimatur. . .et mariti sui miratur arma: notice the alliteration of *m* and assonance of *a*; there is even more clever word-play: *rimatur* and *miratur* are anagrams of one another. Note the emphasis (given extra weight by the possessive *sui*) in calling Cupid her husband; along with *coniugis* at the end of this chapter, Cupid's departure is framed by reminders of their marital relationship.

depromit unam de pharetra sagittam: this section, as it continues, is clearly making reference to the description of the wounding of Venus in Ovid's *Metamorphoses* X.525–8. The tense shifts between the historical present *depromit* and the perfect *pupugit* (from *pungo*); the former is the last in a series of present tenses started with Psyche's contemplation with *videt* in the last chapter; a new series of key perfect tense verbs begins here, describing events which follow in quick, relentless, succession: *incidit. . .evomuit. . .exiluit. . . avolavit.*

punctu pollicis: 'by a pricking of her thumb' (ablative of means). Notice the alliteration of *p*, followed later with *periclitabunda* and *pupugit.*

trementis. . .articuli: genitive, 'of her finger, trembling . . .'

nisu fortiore: ablative of means, 'by a stronger push'.

altius: 'too deep'.

ut. . .roraverint: perfect subjunctive in a result clause. The subject of the clause is *parvulae. . .guttae.*

ignara Psyche sponte: the oxymoron is pointed: Psyche knows exactly what she is doing, but she is oblivious to its consequences.

in Amoris incidit amorem: literally, 'fell into love of Love', i.e. 'fell in love with Love'. Note that *in* goes with *amorem*, not the genitive *Amoris*. This is the first time he is explicitly identified as Love. The play with Cupid's various names are even clearer than the earlier word-play on Psyche's name. Note in a similar vein *cupidine. . .Cupidinis* a little further on.

magis magisque: just like the English idiom, 'more and more'.

cupidine fraglans Cupidinis: literally 'burning with desire of Cupid'; the genitive is best rendered in English 'for Cupid'.

prona in eum efflictim inhians: *in eum* is best translated as 'over him'. The description seems to echo a passage from Lucretius, *De rerum natura* (1.36) where Mars is gazing at Venus: *pascit amore avidos inhians in te, dea, visus* ('he feeds his greedy eyes with love, gaping at you, goddess').

The meaning of *inhians* here is 'gaping', which, like in English, carries both the sense of staring open-mouthed, but also can be used in the original sense of opening the jaws wide to eat: Psyche has become like the devouring beast she feared her husband was.

patulis ac petulantibus saviis...ingestis: ablative absolute, with marked alliteration. *patulis* here might refer to 'open-mouthed' kisses; Walsh translates it as 'wanton kisses from parted lips'. The adjective is also used of the wide-open mouths of predators, however, building on the above suggestion of Psyche as the predator.

de somni mensura: a rather awkward way of expressing the fear that he would wake up; literally 'about the length of his sleep'.

bono tanto percita: nominative participle with an ablative of means. Note that it forms a chiastic construction with the following *saucia mente*, but with the ablatives used in different sense. *bonum* can mean either physical beauty or a more general good.

saucia mente: *saucia* is nominative, followed by an ablative of specification: 'wounded in her mind'. She is described in similar terms in IV.32, but is there *animi saucia* because of her lack of lovers.

lucerna illa: nominative; the subject of the main clause. The personification of the lamp here reaches its climax. *illa* is certainly emphatic, but could be interpreted in different ways: either to denigrate the lamp, as 'that' sometimes does in English; or to draw attention to the key role it is about to play.

sive perfidia. . .sive invidia. . .sive quod tale corpus. . .: the possible motives of the lamp are presented in a tricolon; each of the first two suggestions is in nine syllables, followed by a third colon with twenty-five syllables, just under three times as long. *perfidia* and *invidia* are ablatives of cause, and *quod* = 'because'.

contingere et quasi basiare et ipsa gestiebat: 'it [i.e. the lamp] too was longing to touch, even (as it were) to kiss'. *gestio* is a particularly apt verb to use, suggesting both the agitated movements of Psyche which cause the lamp to spill, and the passionate longing which they represent. The two earlier infinitives (*contingere et quasi basiare*) are dependent on *gestiebat; quasi* (as in the translation here) is almost parenthetical.

de summa luminis sui: 'from the top of its light'; that is, from the opening of the lamp where the wick is actually burning.

hem: an apostrophe to the lamp; it expresses surprise and indignation. With this, the narrator (the old woman in the robbers' cave) enters the story as a speaking character, passing judgement on the role of the lamp. In love elegy, the lamp is usually the silent and appreciated accomplice of the lover; here, its role is reversed as the enemy.

ignis totius deum: 'the god of all fire'. Love and fire are often connected in Greek and Latin literature (as indeed they are in English).

aduris: the address to the lamp continues with this second-person verb.

cum. . .invenerit: should be taken concessively, 'even though. . .', with a perfect subjunctive. The idea of a *primus inventor* is a regular topos in ancient literature – the idea that every art or object must have had a first inventor; it often occurs in comedy and elegy referring to inventions which both help and hinder lovers.

ut diutius cupitis etiam nocte potiretur: purpose clause. *nocte* is ablative of time at which, 'in the night'; it is easiest to translate *etiam* along with *diutius*, 'even longer'.

visaque detectae fidei colluvie: ablative absolute, with an embedded genitive phrase. The genitive is explicative, but the vocabulary used gives space for several interpretations: straightforwardly, 'with the filth of betrayed trust having been seen'; alternatively, *detectae* might refer primarily to his identity which has been 'uncovered'; or it might be an example of hypallage, effectively meaning 'with the revealed pollution of his trust having been seen'.

coniugis: see the note on *mariti* earlier in this chapter.

Chapter 24

The description of Psyche here is dependent on Plato's *Phaedrus* 248c: 'But when [the soul], lacking strength to attend, does not see, and by some misfortune grows heavy, filled with forgetfulness and wickedness, and having grown heavy, it loses its wings and falls to the earth.' See the Introduction, pp. 20–21. As well as philosophical overtones, there is a possible connection to a Greek novel, Longus' *Daphnis and Chloe* (II.7.1) where the two young lovers are told that Love is young and beautiful and winged, and gives wings to souls.

crure dextero. . .adrepto: ablative absolute.

sublimis evectionis adpendix: the genitive is dependent on *adpendix*; i.e. she is an attachment onto his flight. *adpendix* itself is in apposition to *Psyche*; i.e. 'as an appendage', or just 'Psyche. . ., an attachment. . .'

Apuleius is playing with the etymology (from *pendeo*, hang) and the sound of the word by placing it near *penduli*.

miseranda: a gerundive, agreeing with *adpendix*, 'requiring to be pitied', i.e. 'pitiable'.

per nubilas plagas penduli comitatus extrema consequia: *consequia* is nominative (although it is an uncommon word – here and in the vocabulary it is taken as a feminine singular noun, but it could well be a neuter plural used poetically as an abstract noun), as above, in apposition to *Psyche*, with the genitive phrase *penduli comitatus* dependent upon it: 'the furthest rear-guard of his escort'; the prepositional phrase *per nubilas plagas* is dependent on the verbal sense of *penduli*, 'trailing through the cloudy regions'.

The phrase is artificial even for Apuleius; a *comitatus* is a retinue which would accompany an important person everywhere; we are either meant to visualize a literal flying entourage for Cupid, or alternatively read this as metaphor, imagining Psyche as the final hanger-on in a retinue.

solo: 'on the ground'.

deus amator: *amator* is functioning as an adjective here; 'the god who loved her' (GCA). In classical Latin, nouns (especially those ending in *–tor*) could be used adjectivally, and the practice becomes more common in later Latin.

humi: locative, 'on the ground'.

iacentem: sc. *eam* (i.e. Psyche), the object of *deserens*.

involavit...adfatur: Apuleius shifts from the perfect to the historical present in one sentence (not uncommon in the *Metamorphoses*). It can be noted, however, that in this episode, all Cupid's actions are presented in the perfect, and it is only the introduction to the speech which is in the present: so before, we have *exiluit, avolavit,* and after, *se proripuit.* Cf. the note in Chapter 23 on *depromit unam de pharetra sagittam.*

cupressum: accusative following *involavit,* 'he flew into a nearby cypress tree'. Cupid is depicted as perching in trees in Bion (a Greek bucolic poet, *fl. c.* 100 BC), fr. 13(10).3, and in Longus' novel *Daphnis and Chloe,* II.6.1.

Why a cypress in particular? It is the tree associated in Latin literature with death and burial (e.g. Horace, *Odes* II.14); it has been speculated that this may refer to the original folkloric source of the story, in which the spouse died at this point in the tale. Or it might be simply that the cypress is an extremely tall tree: the new distance in their relationship is represented by their physical separation.

graviter commotus: *graviter* carried primarily its metaphorical meaning of 'seriously', but also reminds us of its literal connotations 'weightily'. This is the opposite of the flying, flighty, *levis* Love of literature (e.g. Ovid, *Amores* II.9.49; *Ars amatoria* II.19) and contrasted to his regret later in this passage, *hoc feci leviter*; it also forms part of the intertextual reminder of Plato's *Phaedrus,* echoing the 'growing heavy' of the soul.

simplicissima Psyche: see the note on *simplicitate* in Chapter 11.

parentis meae Veneris praeceptorum immemor: *immemor* takes the genitive *praeceptorum* ('forgetful, not mindful *of*'). This is the first time it is made explicit that Cupid has disobeyed his mother. On the theme of remembering and forgetting, see the note on *praecipiti cum velocitate* in V.14.

te...addici: accusative and (passive) infinitive construction after *iusserat* (which takes an indirect statement rather than an indirect command construction).

devinctam cupidine: 'conquered by desire': a play on words; Cupid has been misled by his lower self. See the Introduction, pp. 20–21. *cupido* has the genitive phrase *miseri extremique hominis* dependent on it, which is more naturally rendered 'desire *for*' in English.

infimo matrimonio: as a phrase (rather than *infimo* with *cupidine*), dependent on *addici*, 'be doomed to the vilest marriage'.

amator: in apposition to *ipse*, 'I myself flew as a lover'.

hoc feci leviter: see above on *graviter*.

scio: parenthetical; i.e. it has no grammatical connection with the rest of the sentence, but expresses Cupid's personal attitude.

praeclarus ille sagittarius: the subject, which is also (as is seen from the verb) Cupid himself, 'I'. The emphatic *ille* highlights the irony of the situation.

ipse me telo meo percussi: the irresponsible use of his weapons was characteristic of Cupid as presented in elegy and Hellenistic poetry; but this (like his admission that he disobeyed his mother) is the first indication to the audience that Cupid has wounded himself with his own arrow.

ut...viderer...excideres: a result clause with imperfect subjunctives. *viderer*, 'with the result that I seemed'; excideres, however, should be understood as imperfect subjunctive representing a future result, '[with the result that] you were going to cut off ...'

quod: relative pronoun, with the antecendent *meum...caput*.

istos amatores tuos oculos: 'those very eyes which are your lovers' (GCA). As in English romantic poetry, eyes frequently occur in Latin love elegy, as the cause or conduit of love. Possibly Apuleius is drawing attention to the recurrent theme of vision throughout the tale.

haec. . .haec: 'these things'; the anaphora, especially with asyndeton, draws attention to the repetition of the warning which Cupid gave, further emphasized by the pleonasm of *identidem semper*; these adverbs are best understood as modifying, respectively, *censebam* and *cavenda*.

tibi. . .cavenda censabam: the gerundive of obligation is neuter plural, agreeing with *haec*, with *tibi* a dative of the agent, with *esse* understood. Literally, 'I was advising that these things [were] requiring to be guarded against by you'; or more naturally, 'I kept on warning that you needed to be on your guard against these things'.

remonebam: an unusual compound; the *re-* prefix suggests repeated warning; it is taking a direct object in *haec* here, 'I kept warning you about these things'.

egregiae: clearly ironic.

tam perniciosi magisterii: genitive, dependent on *poenas* at the end of the clause; smoother in English as 'the penalty *for* . . .'

dabunt. . .mihi poenas: 'they will pay me the penalty', although, as we see later on, it is actually Psyche who avenges herself on her sisters: see V.26–7.

tantum fuga mea: ablative of means; *tantum* is adverbial.

punivero: future perfect; Psyche's punishment he already counts as accomplished once he has left her, and the tense emphasizes this.

cum termino sermonis: 'with the end of his speech'.

in altum: 'into the sky'; cf. the same phrase in V.14 and our note there.

pinnis. . .se proripuit: lit. 'he seized himself forth with his wings'; i.e. he rushed off on his wings.

Vocabulary

While there is no Defined Vocabulary List for A level, words in the OCR Defined Vocabulary List for AS are marked with * so that students can quickly see the vocabulary with which they should be particularly familiar.

*a, ab + abl.	from, by
abdo, abdere, abdidi, abditum	hide, conceal
abeo, abire, abii	go away
abscindo, abscindere, abscidi, abscissum	tear off, divide, cut open
abscondo, -condere, -condi/-condidi, -conditus	conceal
*absum, abesse, afui	be absent
*ac, atque	and
accola, accolae c.	neighbour
*acies, aciei f.	sharpness, point
acquiesco, -ere, acquievi, acquietum	to lie with (+ cum)
actutum adv.	immediately
acumen, acuminis n.	sharpened point
*ad + acc.	to, towards
addico, addicere, addixi, addictum	doom, sentence
adsum, adesse, adfui	be present
adfor, adfari, adfatus sum	address
*adhuc	besides, still
admoneo, -monere, -monui, -monitum	admonish, advise
admoveo, -movere, -movi, -motum	apply
*adolescens, adolescentis m.	young man, youth

adpendix, adpendicis f.	attachment, hanger-on
adrepio, adrepere, adrepui, adreptum	seize
adtexo, -texere, -texui, -textum (also *att-*)	weave to, weave on
adulo, adulare, adulavi, adulatus	fawn, flatter
aduro, adurere, adussi, adustum	burn
advolo, -are, -avi, -atum	fly to (+ dat.)
aestus, aestus m.	tide, surge, swell
aetas, aetatis f.	age
affectus, affectus m.	emotion
affectio, affectionis f.	affection
affero, afferre, attuli, allatum	convey
affirmo, -are, -avi, -atum	affirm, assert, maintain
agito, -are, -avi, -atum	stir
*****ago, agere, egi, actus**	drive, lead, do, perform
ait	says, said
ales, alitis	winged
alimonia, alimoniae f.	nourishment, food
alioquin adv.	in general
*****aliquis, aliquid**	someone, something, anyone, some
ala, alae f.	wing
*****alius, alia, aliud**	other, another
*****alter, altera, alterum**	one/the other (of two)
alterco, altercare, altercavi, altercatus	deliberate, dispute
*****altus, alta, altum**	high, deep
amator, amatoris m.	lover
ambo, -ae, -o irreg.	both
ambrosia, ambrosiae f.	food of the gods, ambrosia
*****amor, amoris** m.	love
amplexus, amplexus m.	embrace, coiling

amplius adv.	further
***an**	whether, or
anceps, ancipitis	two-edged
anhelo, -are, -avi, -atum	breathe out
anima, animae f.	spirit, breath, soul
***animus, animi** m.	soul, mind
***ante** + acc.	before
antependulus, -a, -um	hanging in front
anxius, -a, -um	anxious, worried
apparatus, apparatus m.	supplies, preparation
appello, appellare, -avi, -atum	call, address, call upon
approbo, -are, -avi, -atum	prove
appulsus, appulsus m.	impact, touch
arcus, arcus m.	bow
ardeo, ardere, arsi, arsum	blaze, burn
***arma, armorum** n. pl.	arms, weapons
armatus, -a, -um	armed, equipped
articulus, articuli m.	joint, finger
aspectus, aspectus m.	sight, glance, appearance
assentior, assentiri, assensus sum	comply with (+ dat.)
astus, astus m.	cunning, cunning speech
***at**	but
atque	*see* **ac**
audacia, audaciae f.	boldness, daring
audaciter adv.	boldly
***audax, audacis**	bold, presumptuous
***audeo, audere, ausus sum**	dare
***audio, audire, audivi, auditum**	hear, listen to
aulula, aululae f.	small pot
aura, aurae f.	breeze, air
aureus, -a, -um	golden, of gold
***autem**	but, however
avolo, -are, -avi, -atum	fly away

balnea, balneae f.	bath
barba, barbae f.	beard
basio, -are, -avi, -atum	kiss
beatus, -a, -um	blessed, fortunate, rich
*beneficium, beneficii n.	benefit
benivole adv.	in a spirit of goodwill
bestia, bestiae f.	beast
blandus, -a, -um	flattering, enticing
*bonus, -a, -um	good
*brevis, breve	short
cacumen, cacuminis n.	peak, tip, end
caecus, -a, -um	blind
caesaries, caesariei f.	hair
calamitas, calamitatis f.	disaster
calco, -are, -avi, -atum	trample upon
calor, caloris m.	warmth
candeo, candere, candui	shine, be white
candico, -are, -avi, -atum	have a white appearance, glow
*cano, canere, cecini, cantus	sing
canities, canitiei f.	grey hair
canto, cantare, cantavi, cantatus	sing
cantus, cantus m.	singing
*caput, capitis n.	head
*carus, -a, -um	dear, precious
*castra, castrorum n. pl.	camp
casus, casus m.	fall, overthrow, error
caveo, cavere, cavi, cautum	avoid, be on one's guard against
*celo, celare, celavi, celatus	hide, conceal
celeritas, celeritatis f.	swiftness, speed
censeo, censere, censui, censum	advise

certus, -a, -um	certain, sure
cervix, cervicis f.	neck (often in plural)
ceterum adv.	for, since; for the rest
chorus, chori m.	chorus, group of dancers
cinnameus, -a, -um	(smelling) of cinnamon
circumsecus	round about, in the region around
cithara, citharae f.	cithara (a stringed instrument)
*****clades, cladis** f.	destruction, disaster
*****clamo, clamare, clamavi, clamatus**	shout, pronounce
clandestinus, -a, -um	secret, hidden
claresco, clarescere, clarui	become bright, be illuminated
*****clarus, -a, -um**	clear, bright
classicum, classici n.	trumpet-call, field signal
claudo, claudere, clausi, clausum	shut up, close
*****coepi, coepisse, coeptus**	begin
*****cogito, cogitare, cogitavi, cogitatus**	think, consider
cogitatio, cogitationis f.	thought
*****cognosco, cognoscere, cognovi, cognitus**	recognize, perceive
*****cogo, cogere, coegi, coactus**	force
collum, colli n.	neck
colluvies, colluviei f.	filth
colonus, coloni m.	farmer, inhabitant
color, coloris m.	colour
coluber, colubrum m.	snake, serpent
coma, comae f.	hair
comitatus, comitatus m.	escort
commentum, commenti n.	fabrication, fiction
comminus adv.	hand-to-hand

commoneo, -monere, -monui, -monitum	warn
commoveo, -movere, -movi, -motum	agitate
*comparo, -are, -avi, -atus	prepare
compello, -peller, -puli, -pulsum	compel, force
comperio, comperire, comperi, compertum	ascertain, learn
complector, complecti, complexus sum	entwine around
compleo, complere, complevi, completum	fill full
complexus, complexus m.	embrace
conatus, conatus m.	endeavour, effort
concinnis, -e	ready for use
concolor, concoloris	of the same colour
concubitus, concubitus m.	coupling, lying together
*confero, conferre, contuli, collatus	direct (conversation), join in.
confertus, -a, -um	pressed close, compact
confingo, -fingere, -finxi, -finctum	invent
confinium, confinii n.	proximity
congredior, congredi, congressus sum	fight, contend, approach
*coniunx, coniugis m. & f.	wife
conquiesco, -quiescere, -quievi, -quietum	rest
conscendo, -scendere, -scendi, -scensum	board, embark
consentio, -sentire, -sensi, -sensum	assent, agree with (+ dat.)
consequia, –ae f.	rear guard
consiliatrix, -tricis f.	adviser
*consilium, consilii n.	advice, counsel
conspectus, conspectus m.	view, sight

conspondeo, -ere, -spondi, -sponsum	pledge together
consuesco, -ere, -suevi, -suetum	be accustomed
***contendo, -tendere, -tendi, -tentus**	hasten, march
continentia, -ae f.	self-control
contingo, -ere, -tigi, -tactum	touch
***contra** + acc.	against
***corpus, corporis** n.	body
corrumpo, -rumpere, -rupi, -ruptus	spoil
cresco, crescere, crevi, cretum	grow
crinis, crinis m.	hair (usually in plural)
crucio, cruciare, cruciavi, cruciatum	torture, torment
crus, cruris n.	leg
cubile, cubilis n.	bed
cubo, cubare, cubui, cubitum	rest
cuiatis, cuiatis	of which country, from where
cuius, cuia, cuium	of which, whose
***cum** + abl.	with
***cum**	(connective) when, since
***cunctus, -a, -um**	all, every
cupido, cupidinis n.	desire; as a proper noun, Cupid
cupitum, cupiti n.	desire
cupressus, cupressi m.	cypress tree
***cura, curae** f.	care, concern
curiositas, -tatis f.	curiosity, inquisitiveness
curiosus, -a, -um	curious
***curo, curare, curavi, curatus**	care for, look after
cursus, cursus m.	course
custodia, -ae f.	guard, protection

cutis, cutis f.	surface, skin
*****de** + abl.	down from, from, about
decanto, decantare, decantavi, decantatum	enchant, charm, bewitch
declino, -are, -avi, -atum	avoid
decoriter adv.	becomingly
deduco, deducere, deduxi, deductum	lead, bring away
deficio, deficere, defeci, defectum	to lack (+abl.); to grow faint.
delabor, delabi, delapsus sum	fall
delecto, -are, -avi, -atum	delight, please
delicatus, -a, -um	delicate
denego, -are, -avi, -atum	deny
*****denique** adv.	at last, finally
denubo, denubere, denupsi, denuptum	marry
depromo, -promere, -prompsi, -promptum	draw out
*****descendo, -scendere, -scendi, -scensus**	descend, go down, alight
desido, desidere, desedi, desessum	sink down
desero, deserere, deserui, desertum	abandon, desert
destinatus, -a, -um	determined, fixed
destringo, destringere, destrinxi, districtum	draw, unsheath (a sword)
desum, deesse, defui	be lacking
detego, -tegere, -texi, -tectum	uncover, remove
detergeo, detergere, detersi, detersum	wipe off, wipe away.
deterreo, -ere, -terrui, -territus	be terrified
*****deus, dei** m.	god
devinctus, -a, -um	captivated, conquered
devolo, -volare, -volavi, -volatum	fly down

devoro, -are, -avi, atum	devour, swallow down
devotus, -a, -um	devoted
***dexter, dextera, dexterum**	right
dico, dicare, dicavi, dicatum	dedicate, devote, consecrate
***dico, dicere, dixi, dictus**	say
***dies, diei** m.	day
differo, diferre, distuli, dilatus	hestitate
diffido, diffidere, diffidi, diffisus	despair
***dignitas, dignitatis** f.	dignity, important, honour
diligo, diligere, dilexi, dilectum	love, cherish
dirigo, dirigere, direxi, directum	draw up, arrange
dissimulanter adv.	dissemblingly, secretly
dissimulo, -are, -avi, -atum	hide
distraho, -trahere, -traxi, -tractum	tear apart
***diu** adv.	for a long time
diutius adv.	longer
divinus, -a, -um	divine
documentum, -i n.	proof
***dolor, doloris** m.	grief, sadness
***dolus, doli** m.	trick, fraud
***domus, domus** f.	house, home
dulcedo, dulcedinis f.	sweetness
dulcis, dulce	sweet
***dum**	while, until
***e, ex** + abl.	out of, from
edictum, edicti n.	edict, order
edulia, edulium n. pl.	food
efflictim adv.	desperately
effundo, effundere, effudi, effusum	shed, pour out
egregius, -a, -um	outstanding, excellent
***ego, mei**	I, me
elatus, elata, elatum	raised

ementior, ementiri, ementitus sum	utter falsely
eminus adv.	a spear's throw away, at fighting distance
***enim**	for
***eo** adv.	to such an extent
***eo, ire, i(v)i,**	go
***ergo**	therefore
erogo, -are, -avi, -atum	entreat, successfully implore, win over
***et**	and
***etiam**	even, also, still
evectio, evectionis f.	ascension, flight
evolo, -are, -avi, -atum	fly out, rush out
evomo, evomere, evomui, evomitum	vomit out
exaspero, -are, -avi, -atus	incite
excido, -ere, -cidi, -cisum	cut off
excubo, excubare, excubui, excubitum	to keep watch
exeo, exire, exi(v)i, exitum	go out, exit
exilio, exilire, exilui	leap up
eximie adv.	exceedingly, very much
existimatio, existimationis f.	judgement, opinion
exordium, exordii n.	beginning; warp of a web
exploro, -are, -avi, atum	scout out, reconnoitre
exsanguis, exsangue	drained of blood, pale
extermino, -are, -avi, -atum	exile, banish, expel
extimus, -a, -um	farthest
***extra** + acc.	beyond, outside
extremus, -a, -um	extreme, furthest
facies, faciei f.	form, appearance
facinerosus, -a, -um	villainous, criminal
***facinus, facinoris** n.	crime, outrage, deed

*facio, facere, feci, factus	make, do
factio, factionis f.	faction, conspiracy
faetidus, -a, -um	stinking, offensive
fallacia, -ae f.	deceit, trick, artifice
*familia, familiae f.	family, household
fastidienter	disdainfully, scornfully
fatum, fati n.	fate
fatuus, -a, -um	foolish, silly
*felix, felicis	lucky, happy
*femina, feminae f.	woman
fera, ferae f.	wild beast
*fero, ferre, tuli, latus	bring, bear, carry
*ferrum, ferri n.	iron, weapon, blade
ferveo, fervere	boil, burn
fervidus, -a, -um	hot, glowing
fessus, -a, -um	tired, exhausted
festinanter adv.	hastily
festinatio, -ionis f.	hastening, speed
*festino, -are, -avi	hurry
*fides, fidei f.	faithfulness, faith
fingo, fingere, finxi, fictum	form, contrive, make up
firmitas, firmitatis f.	firmness, constancy
firmiter adv.	steadfastly
flagitium, flagitii n.	shameful act, outrage
flammo, -are, -avi, -atum	inflame
flatus, flatus m.	wind, breath, breeze
fletus, fletus m.	weeping, tears
flo, flare, flavi, flatum	breathe
floreo, florere, florui	flower, blossom
flos, floris m.	flower, brightness
fluctuo, -are, -avi, -atum	be agitated
*flumen, fluminis n.	river
*foedus, foederis n.	treaty, bond

fons, fontis m.	spring, fountain; (poetic) water
forma, formae f.	form
formido, formidinis f.	fear, dread
formonsus, -a, -um	beautiful, handsome
***fortis, forte**	brave
***fortuna, fortunae** f.	fortune, chance
fraglo, fraglare, fraglavi, fraglatum	burn
fraus, fraudis f.	deceit
fructus, fructus m.	enjoyment
***fuga, fugae** f.	flight, escape
fulguro, -are, -avi, -atum	flash
funestus, -a, -um	destructive
fungor, fungi, functus sum	perform, execute (+ abl.)
Furiae, -arum f. pl.	the Furies, goddesses of vengeance
***gaudeo, gaudere, gavisus sum**	rejoice
***gaudium, gaudii** n.	joy, delight
gena, genae f.	cheek
genialis, geniale	delightful
genuinus, -a, -um	natural
germanus, -a, -um	brotherly; genuine, true.
***gero, gerere, gessi, gestus**	bear, wear, carry
gesto, -are, -avi, atum	bear, carry
gestio, gestire, gestivi, gestitum	use passionate gestures, long for
glabellus, -a, -um	without hair, smooth
***gladius, gladii** m.	sword
globus, globi m.	tuft
gloria, gloriae f.	glory
gradus, gradus m.	step
grandis, grande	great
graviter adv.	deeply, seriously
gremium, gremii n.	lap, bosom

gressus, gressus m.	going, trail
gutta, guttae f.	drop
***habeo, habere, habui, habitus**	have
hem	oh! indeed! well!
heu	alas!
hio, hiare, hiavi, hiatum	gape, be eager for
***hic** adv.	here
***hic, haec, hoc**	this
hilaro, hilarare, hilaravi, hilaratum	gladden, cheer
***homo, hominis** m.	man, person
***humus, humi** f.	ground
***iaceo, iacere, iacui**	lie
***iam**	now, already
iamdudum	now for a long time
***idem, eadem, idem**	the same
identidem adv.	again and again
***igitur**	therefore
ignarus, -a, -um	unaware
***ignis, ignis** m.	fire
ignorantia, ignorantiae f.	ignorance
***ignoro, -are, -avi, -atus**	be unaware, disregard
ilico adv.	immediately
***ille, illa, illud**	that, he/she/it
imago, imaginis f.	copy, likeness, image, apparition
immanis, immane	monstrous, immense
immemor, immemoris	forgetful, heedless (+ gen.)
immo	indeed
impeditus, -a, -um	bound
impius, -a, -um	unholy, wicked
implico, implicere, implicui, implicitus	enfold, entangle
impos, impotis	not in control of (+ gen.)

impulsus, -us m.	pressure, influence, blowing (of wind)
imus, -a, -um	deepest
*in + acc./abl.	into, onto/in, on
*incendium, incendii n.	fire, blaze
incertus, -a, -um	uncertain (+ gen.)
incerto, -are, -avi, -atum	render doubtful/inaudible, blur
incido, incidere, incidi, incasum	fall in with
incolumitas, incolumitatis f.	safety
increbresco, -brescere, -brui	increase, prevail
incrementulum, -i n.	small growth
incunctatus, -a, -um	undelaying, without delay
incuria, incuriae f.	carelessness
incuriosus, -a, -um	unconcerned, careless
*inde adv.	from there, next
indulgeo, indulgere, indulsi, indultum	grant
infans, infantis c.	little child, (unborn) baby
infantilis, infantile	child-like, of a child
infelix, infelicis	unhappy, unlucky, wretched
infestus, -a, -um	hostile
infimus, -a, -um	vilest
infirmus, -a, -um	weak
inflammo, -are, -avi, -atum	set on fire, kindle
infortunium, -i n.	misfortune
ingero, ingerere, ingessi, ingestum	put upon
ingluvies, ingluviei f.	gluttony
inhio, -are, -avi, -atum	gape
*inimicus, -a, -um	hostile
innato, innatare, innatavi, innatatum	swim in, float in (+ dat.)
inquietus, -a, -um	restless

insatiabilis, -e	insatiable
*insidiae, insidiarum f. pl.	ambush, trap, trick
insons, insontis	innocent, guiltless
*instruo, instruere, instruxi, instructus	build, equip
*interea	meanwhile
interim	meanwhile
internecivus, -a, -um	murderous
interspersus, -a, -um	sprinkled
intraho, -trahere, -traxi, -tractum	drag in
intueor, intueri, intuitus sum	gaze at, admire
inuro, inurere, inussi, inustum	scorch
invado, invadere, invasi, invasum	invade, attack
*invenio, invenire, inveni, inventus	find, invent
invidia, invidiae f.	envy
*invitus, -a, -um	unwilling
involo, -are, -avi, -atum	fly into
*ipse, ipsa, ipsum	himself, herself, itself
irascor, irasci, iratus sum	become angry
*is, ea, id	he, she, it
iste, ista, istud	that
*ita	in this way
*iter, intineris n.	journey
*iterum adv.	again, a second time
*iubeo, iubere, iussi, iussus	order
iugulum, -i n.	throat
iugum, iugi n.	yoke, pair
*iungo, iungere, iunxi, iunctus	join, unite
lacero, -are, -avi, -atum	mangle
lacrima, lacrimae f.	tear
lacrimosus, -a, -um	tearful
lacteus, -a, -um	milk white
laeto, laetare, laetavi, laetatum	make joyful, delight

*laetus, -a, -um	happy, joyful
lamia, lamiae f.	witch
lanugo, lanuginis f.	down
laqueus, laquei m.	noose, snare
lascivio, lascivere, lascivii, lascivitum	frisk, play
lassus, -a, -um	weary
lassitudo, lassitudinis f.	weariness
latenter adv.	secretly, privately
latibulum, latibuli n.	hiding place, concealment
lectulus, lectuli m.	bed
lenio, lenire, lenivi, lenitus	soften, calm
leviter	thoughtlessly, lightly
*libero, liberare, -avi, -atus	free
licentiosus, -a, -um	unrestrained
*licet, licere, licuit	it is permitted, allowed
locuples, -pletis	fertile, rich
longe adv.	by far
*loquor, loqui, locutus sum	speak; (poetic) make music.
lucerna, lucernae f.	lamp
lucidus, -a, -um	bright, gleaming
lucifuga, lucifugae f.	one who flees daylight
luculentus, -a, -um	brilliant
lumen, luminis f.	light
lupula, lupulae f.	little she-wolf, little whore
luridus, -a, -um	wan, pale
machina, machinae f.	contraption, scheme
maereo, maerere	mourn, lament
*magis adv.	more, rather
magisterium, magisterii n.	instruction
*magnopere adv.	greatly
*magnus, -a, -um	great
*malus, -a, -um	bad, evil

*manus, manus f.	hand, band of men
marcidus, -a, -um	weak
*maritus, mariti m.	husband
*mater, matris f.	mother
maternus, -a, -um	motherly, maternal
matrimonium, matrimonii n.	marriage
maturo, maturare, -avi, -atum	bring to fullness
matutinus, matutina, matutinum	in the morning, early
*medius, -a, -um	in the middle of
mellitus, -a, -um	honey-sweet, lovely
memoria, memoriae f.	memory
mendacium, mendacii n.	lie
*mens, mentis f.	mind
*mensis, mensis m.	month
mensura, mensurae f.	length, depth
mereo, merere, merui, meritum	merit, deserve
merito adv.	rightly
metuo, metuere, metui, metutum	fear
*meus, -a, -um	my, mine
mico, micare, micui	flash, be bright, sparkle
ministerium, ministerii m.	assistant
minuo, minuere, minui, minutum	lessen, diminish
mirus, -a, -um	wonderful
*miror, mirari, miratus sum	wonder, be amazed
misellus, -a, -um	wretched (diminutive)
*miser, misera, miserum	wretched
miseror, miserari, miseratus sum	lament, pity
mitis, mite	gentle
modicus, -a, -um	moderate, short
*modo adv.	just, only just, just now
modulus, moduli m.	measure, melody
molleo, mollere, mollivi, mollitus	to be soft, soften
mollis, molle	tender

momentarius, -a, -um	quick
monitio, monitionis f.	warning
***monstro, -are, -avi, atus**	show, point out, indicate, instruct
monstruosus, -a, -um	monstrous
***moror, morari, moratus sum**	delay, linger
***mos, moris** f.	manner
***mors, mortis** f.	death
mortalis, mortale	mortal
***mox**	soon
mucro, mucronis m.	sword
***mulier, mulieris** f.	woman
multinodus, -a, -um	many-knotted
***multus, -a, -um**	much, many
***munus, muneris** n.	duty, present
***muto, mutare, mutavi, mutatus**	change
mutuor, mutuari, mutuatus sum	obtain, take
***nam**	for
nanciscor, nancisci, nanctus sum	obtain
***nascor, nasci, natus sum**	be born
natales, natalium m. pl.	origin
***navigo, -are, -avi**	sail
***navis, navis** f.	ship
***ne** + subj.	that…not
***nec**	nor, and…not
nefarius, -a, -um	wicked
negotior, negotiari, negotiatus sum	do business, trade
nequitia, nequitiae f.	iniquity, vileness
nescio quis/quid	some(one), a certain
***nescio, nescire, nescivi**	not know, be unaware
nescius, -a, -um	unaware, unknowing
nexilis, nexile	knotted, tied up
nexus, nexus m.	connection, obligation

*nil	nothing
nimius, -a, -um	too much, too great
*nisi	if. . .not, unless
nisus, nisus m.	thrust, push
nocturnus, -a, -um	of the night, night-time
nodus, nodi m.	knot, joint
*nomen, nominis n.	name
*non	not
*nos, nostrum/nostri	we, us
*noster, nostra, nostrum	our
novacula, novaculae f.	razor, knife
*novus, nova, novum	new
*nox, noctis f.	night
noxius, -a, -um	noxious, harmful
nubilus, -a, -um	cloudy
nudo, nudare, nudavi, nudatum	leave exposed
*nullus, -a, -um	no, none
numero, numerare, -avi, -atum	count
*nunc	now
*nuntius, nuntii n.	message, announcement
nuptiae, nuptiarum f. pl.	wedding, marriage
nutrimentum, nutrimenti n.	nourishment; (in the plural) rearing
oblatio, oblationis f.	offering
oblecto, oblectare, oblectavi, oblectatus	please, entertain
*obliviscor, oblivisci, oblitus sum	forget
obsequium, obsequii n.	indulgence, offering, compliance
obstinatus, -a, -um	resolute
occipio, occipere, occepi, occeptus	begin
*oculus, oculi m.	eye
*odi, odisse	hate

*odium, odii n.	hatred
officio, officere, offeci, offectum	come in the way of, obstruct (+ dat.)
*officium, officii n.	duty
oleum, olei n.	oil
*omitto, omittere, omisi, omissus	give up, lay aside
omnino adv.	completely, utterly
*omnis, omne	all, every
onustus, -a, -um	burdened, loaded
opimus, -a, -um	fat, rich, plump, fertile
opiparus, -a, -um	rich, splendid
*oportet, opportere, opportuit	it is necessary, it is proper
opperior, opperiri, oppertus	wait for
opportunitas, -tatis f.	right time
*ops, opis f.	help, wealth
origo, originis f.	source, origin
*os, oris n.	face, mouth
osculum, osculi n.	lips
paeniteo, paenitere, paenitui	repent, be sorry
pallor, palloris m.	paleness
palmula, palmulae f.	little palm
palpebra, palpebrae f.	eyelid
*par, paris	right
parciloquium, parciloquii n.	reserve, discretion (in conversation)
*parens, parentis c.	parent
pario, parere, peperi, partum	bring forth, bear
parricidium, -i n.	horrible crime, murder of a family member
*pars, partis f.	part
parvulus, -a, -um	very small, little, young
pastus, pastus m.	feeding, a feeding ground
pateo, patere, patui	stand open

patulus, -a, -um	wide-open
*paulatim adv.	gradually
paullulatim adv.	little by little, gradually
paveo, pavere, pavi	be terrified
pectus, pectoris n.	breast, heart
*pecunia, -ae f.	money
pedica, pedicae f.	fetter, shackle
pelagus, pelagi n.	sea
pendulus, -a, -um	hanging
penetro, -are, -avi, -atum	penetrate
penitus adv.	deeply, thoroughly
pensilis, -e	hanging
*per + acc.	through
percitus, -a, -um	roused
percutio, percutere, percussi, percussum	pierce
*perditus, -a, -um	ruined, broken, done for
pererro, -are, -avi, -atum	roam over
perfidus, -a, -um	faithless, treacherous
perfidia, perfidiae f.	treachery
periclitabundus, -a, -um	testing (+ acc.)
periclitor, -clitari, -clitatus sum	endanger, put to the test
periculosus, -a, -um	dangerous
*periculum, periculi n.	danger
permaneo, -manere, -mansi, -mansum	keep to, endure (in)
perniciosus, -a, -um	destructive
pernix, pernicis	swift, agile
perpendo, -pendere, -pendi, -pensum	weight carefully
persono, personare, personavi, personatum	sound, make resound
pertrecto, -are, -avi, -atum	busy oneself with, study

perula, perulae f.	little pouch
pervigil, pervigilis	ever watchful, without sleep
pervolo, -volare, -volavi, -volatum	fly (to)
***pes, pedis** m.	foot
pestis, pestis f.	plague
petulans, petulantis	wanton
***peto, petere, petivi, petitus**	seek, pursue, attach
pharetra, pharetrae f.	quiver (of arrows)
pietas, pietatis f.	loyalty
pignus, pignoris n.	pledge, token, guarantee
pinna, pinnae f.	wing
pius, -a, -um	dutiful, pious
***placeo, placere, placui, placitum**	please
plaga, plagae f.	region; expanse of sky
plaudo, plaudere, plausi, plausum	applaud, approve
***plenus, -a, -um**	full
plumula, -ae f.	little feather
***poenas do**	pay the penalty, be punished
pollex, pollicis m.	thumb
***pono, ponere, posui, positus**	place, put
poples, poplitis m.	knee
porrigo, porrigere, porrexi, porrectum	stretch out, spread out
***porta, portae** f.	gate
***possum, potere, potui**	be able
***post** + acc.	after, behind
post adv.	afterwards
posthac adv.	hereafter
***postquam**	after (conjunction)
***potior, potiri, potitus sum**	possess (+ abl.)
***potius** adv.	rather
praeacutus, -a, -um	very sharp

praecaveo, -ere, -cavi, -cautum	be on guard in advance
praeceps, praecipitis	headlong, in a rush, swift
praeceptum, praecepti	order
praecipio, -cipere, -cepi, -ceptum	give an order
praecipito, -are, -avi, -atum	throw headlong
praeclarus, -a, -um	noble, famous
*****praeda, praedae** f.	spoils of way, prey
praeditus, -a, -um	furnished, provided with (+ abl.)
praedico, -dicere, -dixi, -dictum	warn
praegnatio, praegnationis f.	pregnancy
praemico, -are, -avi, -atum	glitter forth
praeminor, -ari, -atus sum	warn in advance
praesens, praesentis	present
praesentia, praesentiae f.	presence
praesidium, praesidii n.	protection, guard, help
praestolor, -ari, -atus sum	stand ready
praeverto, praevertere, praeverti	go before
premo, premere, pressi, pressum	press, overwhelm
pressura, pressurae f.	pressing together
pretiosus, -a, -um	costly, precious
prex, precis f.	prayer, entreaty
pridem	before, previously
*****primus, -a, -um**	first; *cum primum*: as soon as
pristinus, -a, -um	previous, original
*****prius** adv.	first
pro + abl.	in front, for, on behalf of, in return for
*****proelium, proelii** n.	battle
profano, -are, -avi, -atum	desecrate
profero, -ferre, -tuli, -latum	bring forward

*proficiscor, proficisci, profectus sum	set out, depart
profundus, -a, -um	deep, insatiable
proinde	according to
promineo, -minere, -minui	overhang, lean out
promissio, promissionis f.	promise
pronus, -a, -um	leaning forward, inclined
propago, -are, -avi, -atum	increase
propitius, -a, -um	gracious
proripio, -pere, -pui, -reptum	snatch away, hurry away
prorsus	truly, utterly, straight on, forwards
prosilio, -ire, -ivi	leap forward
protinus adv.	straightaway, without pause
provenio, -venire, -veni, -ventum	come from
providentia, -ae f.	providence
provincia, provinciae f.	province
*proximus, -a, -um	nearest, next
psallo, psallere, psalli	to play a stringed instrument
*puella, puellae f.	girl
pulcher, pulchra, pulchrum	pretty
pulchritudo, pulchritudinis f.	beauty
punctulum, punctuli n.	pin-prick
punctus, punctus m.	pricking, prick
pungo, pungere, pupugi, punctum	puncture, prick
punio, -ire, -ivi, -itum	punish
purpureus, -a, -um	purple, dark red
*puto, -are, -avi, -atus	think
Pythicus, -a, -um	Pythian, Delphic (i.e. relating to oracle at Delphi)
*quaero, quaerere, quaesivi, quaesitus	ask, look for, seek
*qualis, quale	what sort of

*quam	how, than, as
quamvis	although
*quantus, -a, -um	how great
*quasi	as if, as it were, just as
*qui, quae, quod	who, which
*quidem	indeed
*ne. . .quidem	not even
quiesco, quiescere, quievi, quietum	rest, keep quiet
*quis, quid	who, what
*quisquam, quaequam, quicquam/quidquam	anyone, anything
quodsi	but if, and if
*quoniam	since, because
*quoque	also
*rapio, rapere, rapui, raptus	seize, carry away
raptim adv.	hurriedly
rarus, -a, -um	rare
recordor, -ari, atus sum	remember, call to mind
recreo, -are, -avi, -atum	restore, refresh
recta adv.	straight away
*recte	rightly, correctly
*reddo, reddere, reddidi, redditus	restore, give back
*redeo, redire, redii	return, go back
*refero, referre, rettuli, -relatus	bring back, render
redintegr, -are, -avi, -atum	renew
redulcero, -are, -avi, -atum	scratch open again
reformo, -are, -avi, -atus	transform, shape again
refoveo, refovere, refovi, refotum	refresh, revive
regalis, regale	royal
religiosus, -a, -um	scrupulous
*relinquo, relinquere, reliqui, relictus	leave behind

remoneo, -ere, -monui, -monitum	warn again, warn repeatedly
remulceo, remulcere, remulsi, remulsum	soothe, delight
repentinus, -a, -um	sudden, hasty
repperio, -ire, repperi, reppertum	find out, discover
requiro, requirere, -sivi, -situm	ask
*****res, rei** f.	thing, issue, matter, affair
*****respondeo, respondere, respondi, responsus**	reply, correspond
resulto, -are, -avi, -atum	reverberate, quiver
resurgo, -surgere, resurrexi, resurrectum	rise again, rise back up
retropendulus, -a, -um	hanging behind
rimor, rimari, rimatus sum	examine
roboro, -are, -avi, -atus	strengthen
roro, rorare, roravi, roratum	drip, moisten
roscidus, -a, -um	wet with dew, dewy
roseus, -a, -um	rosy
rudimentum, -i n.	first lesson, experience
ruina, -ae f.	catastrophe
rus, ruris n.	country
rursum adv.	back, again
sacrilegus, -a, -um	sacrilegious
sacrosanctus, -a, -um	sacred, venerable
*****saepe** adv.	often
saevitia, saevitiae f.	savagery, cruelty
*****saevus, -a, -um**	savage, cruel
sagino, saginare, saginavi, saginatum	fatten, stuff, cram
sagitta, sagittae f.	arrow, shaft
sagittarius, sagittarii m.	archer
saltem adv.	at least, at all events

*salus, salutis f.	safety, salvation
salutaris, -e	saving, salutary
sanguino, -are, -avi, atum	be red, be bloody
*sanguis, sanguinis m.	blood
sarcina, sarcinae f.	package, bundle
*satis	enough, extremely
saucius, -a, –um	wounded
savium, savii n.	kiss
saxum, saxi n.	rock
scelestus, -a, -um	wicked
*scelus, sceleris n.	wicked deed, crime
scilicet	of course, as you know
*scio, scire, scivi, scitus	know
sciscitaor, sciscitari, sciscitatus sum	ask, inquire
scopulus, scopuli m.	cliff, crag
*se, sui	himself, herself, itself, themselves
secretum, secreti n.	secret
secta, sectae f.	path, way of life, class
securus, -a, -um	safe, free from care
*sed	but
*sedes, sedis f.	seat, temple, residence
sedile, sedilis n.	seat, chair
semihians, semihiantis	half-open
*semper	always
senecta, senectae f.	old age
sepelio, sepelire, sepelivi, sepelitum	bury
sequor, sequi, secutus sum	follow, pursue
sermo, sermonis m.	talk, conversation
serpo, serpere, serpsi, serptum	creep, crawl
setius adv.	less

sexus, sexus m.	sex, gender
***si**	if
***sic** adv.	thus
***silentium, silentii** n.	silence
***similis, simile**	like (+dat)
simplex, simplicis	simple
simplicitas, simplicitatis f.	simpleness, innocence
simulo, simulare, simulavi, simulatus	imitate, feign
singultus, singultus m.	sobbing
Siren, Sirenis f.	Siren
***socius, socii** m.	ally
solacium, solacii n.	solace, comfort
solitudo, solitudinis f.	solitude
solitus, -a, -um	usual, accustomed
sollicitus, -a, -um	concerned, worried
***solum, soli** n.	ground
***solus, -a, -um**	alone
***somnus, somni**	sleep
sono, sonare, sonavi, sonatum	sound, make music
sopor, soporis m.	deep sleep
***soror, sororis** f.	sister
sororius, -a, -um	of sisters
sors, sortis f.	lot, prophecy
***spatium, spatii** n.	space, distance
spiro, spirare, spiravi, spiratum	breathe, blow
spiritus, spiritus m.	breath, spirit
splendor, splendoris m.	brilliance
spondeo, spondere, spopondi, sponsum	promise solemnly, pledge
sponte adv.	voluntarily
***statim** adv.	at once
status, status m.	standing, status

*statuo, statuere, statui, statutus	establish, fix
stilla, stillae f.	drip
struo, struere, struxi, structum	draw up, arrange, construct
suadeo, suadere, suasi, suasum	persuade, induce
subaudio, -audire, -audivi, -auditus + dat.	be attentive to
subdo, -dare, -didi, -ditum	to place x (acc.) under y (abl.)
sublimis, sublime	lofty, uplifted
sublimo, -are, -avi, -atus	raise on high, elevate
subministro, -are, -avi, -atum	supply
suboles, subolis f.	offspring
subsidium, subsidii n.	help
subsisto, -sistere, substiti	make a stand, stand by, support
substrepo, -ere, -strepui	mutter, whisper
sulco, -are, -avi, -atum	furrow
*sum, esse, fui	be
summa, summae f.	essence
*summus, -a, -um	the top of, highest
*sumo, sumere, sumpsi, suptus	take up, take
super + acc.	on top of
supplex, supplicis	suppliant, entreating, humble
sursum adv.	on high
*suscipio, suscipere, suscepi, susceptus	take up
suspendo, -pendere, -pendi, -pensus	hang
*suus, -a, -um	his, her, its, their
*tacitus, -a, -um	silent
taeter, taetra, taetrum	foul, loathsome
*talis, tale	such
*tam	so

*tamen	however
*tandem adv.	after some time, at last
tantillus, -a, -um	so small a quantity
*tantum adv.	just
*tantus, -a, -um	so great, such a great
tegmen, tegminis n.	covering
*tego, tegere, tegi, tectus	cover, hide
*telum, teli n.	weapon
temerarius, -a, -um	reckless
temeritas, temeritatis f.	recklessness, rashness
*tempus, temporis n.	time
temulentus, -a, -um	drunk
tenax, tenacis	tenacious
tenebra, tenebrae f.	darkness
tenellus, -a, -um	tender; diminutive of *tener*.
*teneo, tenere, tenui, tentus	hold, possess
tener, tenera, tenerum	tender, soft
teneritudo, teneritudinis f.	tenderness
teres, teretis	smooth
terminum, termini n.	end
*terreo, terrere, terrui, territus	frighten, terrify
tertio, -are, -avi, -atum	stammer
thesaurus, thesauri m.	treasure, treasury
tibia, tibiae f.	shin-bone, flute, pipe
*timor, timoris m.	fear
titubo, -are, -avi, -atum	falter
tolero, -are, -avi, -atum	endure
torus, tori m.	bed
*totus, -a, -um	whole, entire
*traho, trahere, traxi, tractus	drag
tranquillus, -a, -um	calm, peaceful
tremo, tremere, tremui	shake, tremble
tremulus, -a, -um	trembling

trepido, trepidare, -avi, -atum	be afraid
triclinium, triclinii n.	dining room
***tristis, triste**	sad
trux, trucis	wild, savage
tuccetum, tucceti n.	a kind of haggis, delicacy
***tu, tui**	you
tunc	then
turbo, -are, -avi, -atum	agitate, disturb
turgidus, -a, -um	swollen
***tuus, -a, -um**	your
***ultimus, -a, -um**	last, final
umerus, umeri m.	shoulder
unda, undae f.	wave
undique adv.	on all sides
***unquam**	ever
unus, una, unum	one
urgueo, urguere, ursi	press upon, beset, bear hard
***ut**	(+ subj.) so that, that, (+ indic.) as, when, how
uter, utra, utrum	which of two
uterus, uteri m.	womb
utpote	as
vacillo, -are, -avi, -atum	waver, falter
vadum, vadi n.	shallow, shoal, ford
***validus, -a, -um**	strong, powerful
vaporosus, -a, -um	steaming
***vehementer**	forcefully, very much
vehiculum, vehiculi n.	carriage, transport
***vel**	either, or
velitor, velitari, velitatus sum	skirmish
velocitas, velocitatis f.	speed
veneno, -are, -avi, -atum	imbue with poison, infect with poison

venenum, veneni n.	poison
venor, venari, venatus sum	hunt, go hunting
*****ventus, venti** m.	wind
ventosus, -a, -um	windy
*****verbum, verbi** n.	word
*****vero** adv.	truly
*****verus, vera, verum**	true
vesania, vesaniae f.	madness
*****vespera, vesperae** f.	evening
vestigium, vestigii n.	footstep
*****vester, vestra, vestrum**	your
*****via, viae** f.	way, street
vicis, vicis f.	change; **in vicem**: in place of, instead of
*****video, videre, vidi, visum**	see; (in passive) seem
vigilia, vigiliae f.	wakefulness, sleeplessness
vilis, vile	worthless
vipereus, -a, -um	of a serpent, snake-like
*****vir, viri** m.	man
virus, viri m. n.	poison, venom, virus
*****vis, vires** f.	strength, might
viscera, viscerorum n.	innards, heart
*****vivo, vivere, vixi**	live, be alive
vocalis, vocale	voice-filled
volatilis, -e	winged, fleeting
*****volo, volere, volui**	want, wish
volumen, voluminis n.	coil
votivus, -a, -um	longed-for
*****vox, vocis** f.	voice
*****vultus, vultus** m.	face, expression
Zephyrus, Zephyri m.	the West Wind (personified as a god)

not
masc